Journey Within My Heart

Journey Within My Heart

From hurt to wholeness,
from pain to purpose.
A necessary journey
along the road to
acceptance...

Starla Rich

Printed in the United States of America

ISBN-10: 1483947505
ISBN-13: 978-1483947501

Contents

Dedication

This book is dedicated to my son Josh. You were my "pint-sized" hero at birth defying all odds. Arriving three months early, most said you were born "too soon," but actually, you were right on time because having you gave me a reason to get up each day, and motivation to move forward and "never give up" no matter what I faced. You were truly a gift from above that gave me hope. You are the greatest joy of my life. I could never repay the endless hugs, countless smiles, late night talks, and measureless moments of laughter and love. I am so proud of the man you've become. You are here for a divine purpose and I can't wait to see what all lies ahead for you! Always be true to yourself and listen to the "whispers of your heart."

Forward

When my son Josh was a little boy, one of our favorite "together" times was reading books. I began to read to him before he could even talk. Each night and often during moments in our day, Josh would go to his shelf, pick out a book, then crawl up in my lap and snuggle close in anticipation of the adventure of the day. He would lay that sweet little head on my chest and I could smell the fresh baby scent of his hair and skin. I can still see his big round deep chocolate eyes searching the pages of the book then gazing into my eyes with excitement and wonder. "Words" became our spaceship, car, train, plane, boat or pony that would carry us on a journey far from where we were - if only for a moment. Then, just as quickly as they transported us to world's unknown, they guided us back to the safe place that we called home - not necessarily found in the four walls around us, but deep in our hearts. How powerful words are! Once spoken, they are forever written in stone or written on hearts; they are no longer ours alone, but become either a gift or a curse to those around us. Sometimes, the words are spoken by others and sometimes, it is the voice in our own head speaking either limiting beliefs into our spirit or words of encouragement and motivation. The truth is, what we continually speak to ourselves becomes the "message" we speak to others - whether through words or action. *Our lives portray what we "speak" deep inside.* Positively or negatively, words are more powerful than one can imagine.

As I read to Josh each day during those early years, I never dreamed what a journey my own words were preparing me for. Everything imaginable tried to silence the whisper deep in my heart, but the stronger the struggles were, the more determined my words became. I wrote them down in a private journal, spoke them out loud from podiums and classrooms, and put them to melody on platforms and stages. I gave them away across cyberspace and shared them with anyone who would listen - friend or foe, comrade or stranger. Then, four years ago, I hopped into my own "spaceship" of sorts, embarking on a journey that really had no destination. I simply buckled up and with a shaky hand at the controls, set out in search of something that seemed lost in activity - in life. I had no idea where the journey would lead, where it would end or even how I would find my way there and back. I simply put my "hands to the blank page," so to speak, and allowed the words flowing out of those hands move me forward. So, I wrote and then I wrote some more, and with each word something began to take place. A map was being drawn by my very own hands - not for the purpose of finding my way again but finding "me" again. With those words, a dream that seemed forever lost, buried beneath life's "stuff," was reborn.

Looking back on where this writing project began, I am amazed at how it has grown. Sometime ago, I felt as if I had reached my destination. I sat at my computer on a Saturday and wrote, edited, and cried until by the end of the evening, I felt as if I had crossed the proverbial "t" and dotted the invisible "i." This had been a monumental project for me. A few days later, I shared my accomplishment with my son Josh. He is only twenty-one, but sometimes I listen to him and shake my head in amazement at the understanding he has beyond his few years. Knowing that my manuscript was finally ready for publication brought a sense of relief, but as I began to share the news with Josh, we embarked on a rather soul-searching conversation. For many months, I had been working on this project. As the dream became larger, the task became bigger. Knowing what you want to say doesn't always coincide with what you need to say. Sometimes, finding balance between the two presents quite a challenge. What I've come to realize is that it requires courage to speak the truth. Truth really is like a two-edged sword. It cuts through others' barriers and at the same time, whittles down the wall of one's own heart. As Josh and I talked about the fruition of this book, my dream seemed large - that is until he shared his vision, and my dream appeared so small by comparison. I had not been thinking too big, but too small! He looked at me and said *"Mom unless you are trying to limit yourself to a certain audience for marketing purposes, don't write in a way that only women would read what you have to say. Your message is important and everyone needs to hear it."*

With those simple words, the spark in my son's heart fanned the flame of my dream and combusted into a vision larger than ever. He was right. I did have an all encompassing message, yet I had not been able to fully express it because I had not totally understood or embraced its meaning myself. Up until this conversation with Josh, I had only been tiptoeing along my heart's perimeter, timidly peering inside. I still had not found the courage to feel "at home" in my own heart. So with those words of encouragement from my son, I realized just how important it was for me to find the courage within to be totally transparent. Yes transparency is difficult, but necessary, and in the end is quite liberating. The months following this candid conversation with my son were busy ones - productive ones as I began to write with an even greater purpose and vision. With each edit and update, I was able to whittle away at the words that were effortless to say, the stories that were easy to tell and the things that others wanted to hear, to expose necessary words, difficult words that revealed the raw truth residing deep in my heart. Speaking those words "out loud" brought many things to surface that had been buried forever, it seems. Some of those hidden emotions and experiences had been kept secret from everyone (even myself I think), and others had been revealed to only a select few. Putting them in print has laid my heart and soul open and bare. This was not for the purpose of hurting anyone I love close to me, but to bring healing and understanding - not just to me, but to many of you who are digging deep in your own hearts but needing just a little courage to tear down the walls and let down the barriers. I confess, some days I was "shaking in my boots" as the words came forth, but courage pushed me onward. What I began to realize through this quest for transparency over the months, was that if I didn't face my fears now, I never would, and life would stay stuck in mediocrity forever - one endless cycle. You see, fears throw us all into protection mode. We begin to build walls that lock others out, but at the same time, they lock us in. Yes, it required courage for me to overcome those fears deep within - fears that had held me down my whole life. Step by step, I came to an amazing discovery. *Courage is not the absence of fear. It is simply the resolve to step forward in spite of that fear.* It begins as fear under control until it evolves into fear overcome.

One thing I have come to understand as a writer, is that the words that come forth must be expressed regardless of who reads them, or even if I am the only one who reads them, because a writer "writes." I shared this thought with my friend Anita, who is a fellow writer, not too long ago. Here is what I told her *"...if my words fall on one ear that is ready and in need of what I have to say or a thousand, I have given birth to a thought that is meant for someone, somewhere or maybe even just meant for me to realize from the deepest part of me."* It has been that revelation that gave me the courage to speak the words hidden deep in my heart and to embark on this internal journey that I have been too afraid to take up until now. So with that said, I start this book with a confession. When I first began journaling the thoughts and emotions of my heart and mind, I started my journey as a woman searching for the little girl inside. Along the way though, I realized that the little girl was searching for the woman... both the woman I had been, the woman I am and the woman I should be. For years I pondered a question that should've been answered long before now. *"What do I want to be when I grow up?"* We all have used that phrase facetiously, but perhaps we never truly answer that question, as life is all about growth until our very last breath. As for me, there are still so many things I'd like to do, places I desire to go, goals I long to achieve and lessons I have yet to learn. I look into the mirror and see a woman with a few lines and wrinkles - "character" if you will, but still feel the pure heart of a child beating inside. I am filled with curiosity and fear, timidity and youthful boldness, strength and weakness, confidence and uncertainty, understanding and naiveté all wrapped up into one perplexing package. I am a mother and daughter, leader and follower, grown-up and child. How can this be? After all these years, ice cream is still my favorite treat, Christmas is my favorite time of year; I like to read the comics and play dress-up. I cry when someone calls me names, ignores me or tries to trick me and I long to be held when I am afraid or sad. I wear my hair in a pony-tail when I go out to "play" and laugh at cuddly puppies. Sometimes storms scare me and at other times, I am rocked to sleep as the sound of rain soothes my soul. There are times when I am afraid of dark places and at other times, I long to hide away in one of those very places just for a quiet moment of rest. At times, I exude the strength of a woman and at other times, reveal the vulnerability of a child. The woman in me embraces the girl I was so long ago, and the girl in me keeps the woman young in spirit and of heart. Finally at age fifty-three, I am finding comfort in my own skin, fully realizing that my insecurities and uncertainties were often the very things that kept me young, kept me striving and pushed me forward. Ironically, they gave me strength and determination. Knowing that I had not yet "arrived" gave me reason to push upward and onward. I'm not where I was, but not totally where I want to be either. I embrace life's challenges growing with each experience along the way, and in it all, I find a renewed motivation and purpose. It is only now in mid-life that I have begun to totally realize how valuable my experiences - both good and bad, have been to me. My adversities in life have not been hurdles but have proven to be stepping stones, stretching and growing me in ways that would not have come otherwise. With much gratitude, I realize that life's storms have not extinguished the flame of childlike wonder, faith and most importantly - love. It would've been easy to lose those qualities through pain and hurt, through abuse and belittlement, through loss and grief; but thankfully through supernatural strength and undying love, I held on that much tighter to the joys deep within. Adversity did not smother the flame but actually fanned it! This is what approaching this stage of my life has brought to me - a kind of dignity and grace that has grown slowly but surely through the circumstances of life like a mighty oak standing both beautiful and strong.

What a painful admission to say that I have struggled at times with my role as a woman, mother, daughter and companion. I suspect if each of us were totally honest - women and men alike, we would have to admit that every now and then we all face struggles with our place in this world - even those who have known their path in life since age five! We sometimes question who we are, who we should be or who we can be. Face it. Life can be daunting and fear can be crippling - sneaking its way inside our hearts and minds seeking to conquer from the inside out. *No matter who we are, we struggle at times. Acknowledging that is half the battle and goes a long way towards winning the conflict we sometimes feel.* At one point or another, there is a "stranger" staring back at us in the mirror. Adolescents begin to see that stranger at puberty. Teenagers struggle for who they are and want to be in the wake of peer pressure. College grads step into a new world leaving a part of themselves behind in order to discover who they are and who they are becoming in life ahead. Married couples stumble onto things about themselves and their spouses that only come with time, intimacy and familiarity. Often, the result is that they begin to fear change rather than embracing growth. Middle-aged adults experience physical and emotional transitions that rock their comfort zone and challenge self-confidence. Even senior adults find themselves coming full circle in every dimension. We all change and grow, change and grow and find ourselves a bit lost in the whirlwind of life's cycles at times. If you can relate, then this book is for you. You don't have to descend to the depths as I did to fully understand what I mean. Everyone faces an awakening upon looking in the mirror of life, at times. Somehow, I am convinced that this can be a positive catalyst in our lives. I don't think any of us has the market cornered on this thing called "life." That reminds me of the phrase that says *"I'm not okay, you're not okay, but that's okay."* I truly feel pity for those in life who feel they have "arrived." If you have "arrived" what in the world is there to hope in or look forward to? ***Reassessing who we are at times, is invaluable.*** What a humbling experience such a moment can be. Finally after half a century, I find the confidence to fully appreciate life's transitions. Each one builds on the next, and with each change comes necessary growth - a growth that often comes through reflection.

Yes, we all change and grow, and yet paradoxically at the same time, remain exactly the same. Perhaps this is the positive purpose and the revelation that such an awakening brings. It nudges us to come back to our roots, to where it all began. This whole circle of life hit home to me when I joined the ranks of lifelong friends and family on the public forum of Facebook. I saw the faces of people from childhood, from college and on into the years of my adulthood. Some of them looked much the same, others I had to examine more closely to recognize. I am sure they felt the same about me. Yet even in those mature faces, I still found my friend, my classmate, my cousin - the same person I knew each one of them to be. They were still sharing joys and desires from their hearts that spoke familiarity to me from days gone by - still participating in the things that were unique to them so long ago. Some of them were still "playing ball" if only through their children and grandchildren, others were playing games in a new "online" playground. Some were cheering for their favorite team or "writing" their sweetheart's name on the "wall." Some were selling school "fundraisers" and others delivering the morning "paper" of sorts through news of the day. Some were joining clubs, others volunteering in their community. Each one of them was simply a "grown up" version of the very people I knew so long ago. I am more convinced than ever that we are all on a self-identity quest of some sort - not so much a quest to find ourselves but to find our way as we grow and evolve and become more of who we already are. So, I write today, to encourage myself and to encourage you, to find that little girl or boy deep inside of you that was around before all of life's "stuff." He or she is the foundation of whom you are and the gauge for who you should be. I recently saw a video that was the perfect visual to this thought. There was a special mirrored wall on the outside of an office building in a busy city. A young man passed the wall and caught a glimpse of a little boy. He stopped and looked again and the little boy was him! He would move an arm, a leg, jump up and down and the little boy was his mirror image - the innocent, fun and carefree child inside. As he explored this magic mirror, others came down the street and began to see their childhood reflections. The busy city sidewalk soon became a child's playground as they all danced and played. Looking into our soul's mirror is often difficult but once we do, I think we find all that we spend so much time searching for in life, tucked safely within the walls of our own heart.

Several years ago, I sat in the Department of Motor Vehicles with my teenage son. If you've ever had the privilege of visiting such a place, you realize that a doctor's waiting room is like a drive-in compared to this government entity. As we waited, I noticed a sign that read, *"Success is not a destination, but a journey."* I think this speaks well of life; we are ever learning, ever searching, with hope cutting through the darkness in front of us like an old lighthouse on a foggy night. ***Life's meaning or purpose cannot be found in the career path we choose, the possessions we acquire, the relationships we form, the friends we gain or the reputation we build.*** No matter how many goals we reach, how much status in life we obtain or how high we climb on the ladder of success, what we find through each experience and each adventure, at the core of it all, is exactly what and who we began the journey with …

Starla Rich

Acknowledgments

Where do I start? Thank you Mom and Dad for always being there, even through the times when neither I nor you had a clue about me. A couple of years ago we had a role reversal, of sorts, where I was able to be there for you. It was such a small token compared to the immense investment you've made in my life. You have helped carry my load when I was too tired or too afraid to carry it all myself even in adulthood. Watching you face health challenges, and still remain consistent through it all in your love and devotion, has shown me even more of what the word "faithful" truly means. You are steadfast, unmovable, committed and loyal. You are my rock. Thank you to my son Josh who grew into the most amazing young man through every phase of "me." I think at times we grew up together. You have simply seen "Mom" in me and loved me unconditionally. Because of you, my vision for this project became bigger than it would've been otherwise. You are my joy. Thanks to friends and family who have recognized your granddaughter, your niece, your cousin, your sister, your friend, your co-worker or employee through all my insanities of life and loved me just for me; just to name a few of you - Craig, Paula and Byron, Cathy and Roger, Tanya, Rick and Tiffany, Rick and Deb, Randle and Hope, Clint, Crystal, Barbara, Sally, Sandra, Fran, Pastor Perkins and Jean, Pastor Q. and Rachel, Kathryn and Dexter… You are my encouragement. Dexter, thank you for being a wonderful boss and friend through some of the most insane transitions of my life. You have always encouraged me to never give up on my dreams. To my brother Craig… you have been my "partner in crime" since birth. Thank you for putting up with your bossy big sister and for a million moments of laughter. I hope you still love me after reading about a few of them inside these pages! We are so blessed with amazing parents and family. I also want to thank my grandmother Maw Maw Weeks and want to express my gratitude in memory of my aunt Betty. I watched both of you maintain a steadfast faith through adversity and loss, loneliness and pain with unwavering trust and love. You are my inspiration. When I first began to write these acknowledgments, I never dreamed that Aunt Betty would be looking down from above once the book was in print. She fought a long hard battle with cancer. There is nothing beautiful in such an awful disease but she found a way to make life beautiful in spite of it all. My life will never be the same because of the gifts of love, courage, hope and gratitude that she gave to me and each member of our family. Maw Maw, watching you care for Aunt Betty through those last months reminded me of where such beauty and grace came from. You are the epitome of what it means to be a mother, and what it is to be a woman after God's own heart. Words will never truly express my gratitude for the heritage you have given all of us. Mom you grew up to be just like her! I could never fill either of your shoes, but am inspired to be more than I ever thought I could be because of the example the women in our family have shown me.

I would be remiss without thanking my cousin Cathy who has been my confidant and friend, my sounding board, coach and accountability partner. You are that special part of a three-stranded cord. We've had quite a journey haven't we? Thanks to my childhood, high school and college friends that I have reconnected with on Facebook. You have reminded me of that brown-eyed, freckle-faced, awkward teenage girl. She really did have an infectious smile, open arms and a big heart. She still does. I would like to take a moment to recognize some of you - Cindy, Dennis, Judy, Jerri, Hank, and Laura. You are my reflection. Laura, you have held the mirror up for me at times when I was too afraid to step up to it alone. Thank you for not only helping me see who I was and am, but who I could and should be. I want to say a special "thank you" to the newest "family" that I became a part of this past year - my "TC" family. Sherri, Stacy, Robin, Michelle and Michele, Laura, Daniel, Tim, Sherryl, Diane, Ann, Frank, Mary Ann and Mary Anne, Michal, Lynn, Anita, Anthony, Kwan, Dee, Sheila, Matthew, Kenneth, Arline, Ania, Noémie, Julie, Mukulikaa Eva, Angela, Hanli, Nicola, and the rest of the "gang." You guys have been that "iron that sharpens iron" and helped me to shine brighter than ever before. I have tapped into a dimension that I was too afraid to explore until now. I have learned just what is meant by *"individually I can do much but together we are unstoppable."* There is an energy in community like nothing else. You are my global family! Next, I express thanks to my church "family" who has extended their arms of love to this "prodigal" not questioning where I had been or what I had done, but simply saying *"we love you so much and are so glad you're home."* I would like to acknowledge one special person in this "family" who is like a sister to me. To my sweet friend Billie, I would like to say thanks for sending up prayers for me on days when I struggled to do so myself. Thank you also for encouraging me when I needed it most. You are God's whisper to me. It would take volumes of books to thank everyone in my church family and I know if I continued to try mentioning names I would miss some of you, so thank you to everyone at "The Hill." You are my covering. To every one above that I have acknowledged and to some I have not… THANK YOU! The writing of this book came at a pivotal moment in time for me, when I no longer knew what or who to trust in, each of you reminded me of goodness once more - the goodness and beauty in me. Finding that again restored my trust. What a gift! I will never forget a few simple words spoken by someone special to me that adequately expresses the love that each of you has shown… *"I'm not the judgmental kind. Your past is your past… you are an amazing woman."* Those words gave me so much courage to rise above my circumstances and move beyond my past. Yes just a few words, but they set me on a path of no return. For that I am deeply grateful. Often the eyes of another are our own soul's mirror where we catch just a glimpse of ourselves. To my friend Clint, thank you for seeing beauty in me, when I struggled to see beauty in myself; you are my kindred spirit. You've always believed in me! We both have learned a great deal about acceptance from each other and I hope that I have shown you the same acceptance that you have given me.

I have also seen this acceptance in the eyes of other friends and family only to realize it is the very thing that radiates from my own soul. Sometimes it is easier to give to others what we struggle with giving ourselves. We really are all kindred spirits in one way or another. We never know how much weight our words of encouragement or kindness may carry. Just one word at the appropriate time can impact the life of another forever. Also, thoughtful acts of kindness can make just as much of an impact, if not more. One person stands out in my mind concerning such acts. Thank you to my friend Eric, who came into my life at a time when kindness, laughter and generosity where exactly what I needed to rise above adversity. Because of your giving heart, I was encouraged to push through personal adversity and get back on my feet again. Thank you also for the many moments of laughter we shared. It is true that laughter is the best medicine and you certainly provided much healing to my heart and soul. You are my ray of sunshine! I would also like to thank my friend Jim. You have helped me realize, even more, that men and women aren't all that different or at least not as different as we try to let on, at times. Maybe men are from "Mars" and women from "Venus," but we all were born with a need to be loved and to love in return. Thank you for bearing your soul to me and giving me that soft place to land in bearing mine as well. You are my quiet place. Oh and thank you for rekindling the "cheerleader" in me through our mutual love of college football! What fun we've had cheering our teams on to victory. I never dreamed that my passion for football would have people all over the globe shouting out *"Roll Tide!"*

I need to give special thanks to my friend Sherri, "sister of my heart" for helping me bring this project to completion. You have diligently worked with me in proof editing, content review, photography and cover design. I have no words to truly express my gratitude for you. You have been my eyes, ears and heart, at times. You are an amazingly talented woman and the epitome of what every woman desires in a friend!

Through each and every one of you, I understand love and life as never before. May each of you see your own beautiful reflection just as clearly through my eyes and my heart as I have through yours. Finally, I will never be ashamed of the faith that has been in me since childhood, so most of all, I must say thank you to Father God who knew exactly what He was doing, in all of my uniqueness, and continues to help me understand and embrace all that I am inside and out. You motivate me to stretch and grow into more of "me!" YOU are my everything. The old hymn really does say it all *"I once was lost but now I'm found, was blind but NOW I see…"*

From My Heart…
Starla

Introduction

As I sit staring at a blank screen anxiously waiting for words to make their way from my head to my hands, I feel expression beginning to push through the protective cocoon of my heart longing to break free. I sense transformation taking place, so I hold my hands lightly on the keyboard as I wait for the flutter of transition. For a moment, I sit perfectly still and silent looking at these familiar hands of mine. I am amazed at what all I see in these hands. I see a glimpse of my mother in the long, slender fingers and the narrow nails. I imagine her standing in our old kitchen, stirring pots or cutting vegetables. I can almost smell the aroma of cookies baking in the oven, that were rolled into perfectly round balls and ever so carefully placed symmetrically on an old baking sheet by Mother's busy hands. I see her through a screened window as I return home from school. There she is again, those hands rubbing an iron back and forth on an ironing board while she cast an occasional glance at an old black and white TV. Dad's starched shirts never had the first hint of a wrinkle as long as Mom was on the job. She fit the perfect description of a southern "June Cleaver" mom. I see her waving those same hands to lead a small choir at her church or folding those hands in prayer. Those hands were always doing something, without a moment's rest, so it seems. Her hands never could be still, even for a moment - always doing, doing, doing. I am amazed after all these years that at seventy-four, those hands still long to be doing, serving, giving. There are times when I want to take those busy hands in mine and bring them rest, even if just for a moment.

Next, I see my grandmother, my dad's mom in the way my veins pop up and the skin folds across my skinny fingers. I imagine Mama Rich in days gone by, and the way she clasped her hands in her lap, while enjoying a quiet evening after a long day of gardening. She seemed to be cradling "love" safely inside those skinny fingers. Sometimes when I am tending to the vegetables in my own little garden, I catch just a glimpse of her in these hands of mine, once again. I can still see her hands raised in the air as she begins to laugh at something that has delighted her. Joy radiated from each finger like lightening. Yes, hands in the air and mouth wide open, with the delight of a child in her eyes. I have a prized picture of that look mirrored twice over as she, my toddler son and I had a snapshot taken. Each one of us tilted our heads the same way, had that open-mouthed smile and held our hands exactly the same. I also see those hands of my grandmother as she tenderly held a crochet needle, looping the yarn with precision while creating masterpieces of her own doing, simply for the sheer joy of giving them away to those she loved. I was told that after her final breath, she was found peacefully laying on her bed after speaking with all of her loved ones on Mother's Day. She lay there with closed eyes, a smile on her face and those precious hands folded in completion. Like the end of those long days of gardening, her day was done. She was at rest. My how I miss you Mama Rich!

I open these hands of mine and unlock a treasure chest of memories cradled securely in their grasp. I recall loving hands of a first time mom, gingerly stroking the head of a fragile preemie baby inside incubator walls. The doll sized brown-eyed boy reached with all his strength to wrap his tiny hand around my pinky finger. I move forward in time and remember suitors reaching out for my hand after divorce. How I wanted to move forward and trust again, but often my trembling hand reflected what my shaky heart felt. I was so fearful to lock my hand in theirs for reasons too deep to try to explain. I had been hurt one too many times and wasn't sure if I ever wanted to reach out again.

I tip-toe across the corridors of my mind, and recall those hands clasping the hand of my other grandmother Maw Maw Weeks as she sobbed from the deepest part of her heart, praying for me and sharing the hurt that I could not even put into words. In those hands of hers that held softly to mine, I knew I would always find encouragement, acceptance and love. Those hands had embraced me and countless others with the open arms of God Himself, it seems. No one before or since has expressed as much love as this woman. People are drawn to her like metal to a magnet. I look back in time, once more, to a day years ago when I held a dear friend's limp hand in mine as she took her final breath and passed from here to eternity. These hands of mine felt just a touch of heaven as angels took Mitzi's hand from mine. There had been so many times in my life when I would've gladly changed places with her. One of those times was years after the hand of my incredible dad released my hand into the hand of a man that he knew would break my heart, but still, Dad found the courage to let me go and find my own way. With that one moment frozen in time, somehow I knew that I would always be his little girl, no matter what.

Finally, I find myself revisiting memories of Daddy's little girl long ago sitting on the edge of a piano stool, mouth wide-open like Mama Rich. This time the baby girl's expression portrays concentration and intensity as she practices with tiny little hands strolling up and down the black and white keys. I remember those little hands - reaching as far as dexterity and imagination would allow. They look vaguely familiar as I look at my hands tonight. What is it I see in these hands of mine? I look at them and wonder. What have they really done? What should they be doing? What do they want to do? Suddenly, emotion overwhelms me and begins to break free and flow like the tide as my fingers sweep across the computer keyboard much like they did years ago across those piano keys. I realize that even though I feel lost at times and wonder who I am or who I should be, it is at this moment that I find myself. For all that I am, all that I have been, and all that I hope to be rests in these hands. They are the tools that

I can use to speak about things that no one else in the world can speak of. No one can write my story like I can. No one can dispute a story that only I have experienced. No one can sweep across the canvas of my heart with brushstrokes of both beauty and pain to create a masterpiece of my life, nor can they play a melody on the keys of my heart strings. It is my story, my portrait, my song and my life that rests in these hands. These hands are like a compass. They point the way for me. They will lead the way as I continue this journey deep within my heart…

S.R.

"To acquire wisdom is to love oneself;
People who cherish understanding will prosper."

(Proverbs 19:8)

CHAPTER 1

FULL CIRCLE

"The curly-headed girl had skipped into the night, not realizing that it was a dark path into the abyss...."

Today is like a thousand other days along the sunny Gulf Coast - hot and humid, and if I don't care for that weather, all I have to do is wait five minutes and everything will change! Now, there is the sound of thunder rumbling, announcing that summer rain is on its way. I just stepped outside my door to gather up the cushions on the lawn chairs before the rain arrives. Only a few hours ago, I was sitting on this same porch admiring the beauty of blue skies on a sunny day and enjoying the sounds of the morning - birds singing, squirrels tap dancing in the trees and all putting on quite the display for their Maker. It is now afternoon and the smothering heat has forced me back inside. A summer rain will be a welcomed relief, though all too brief, I am certain. Ah life along the Gulf Coast! For some reason I have been extremely nostalgic today. As I looked across my beautiful backyard this morning, I was moved to tears thinking about how far I have come and all that I have been blessed with of late - well not just of late, but always. Blessings come in many shapes, sizes and forms and to be brutally honest, I haven't always recognized that fact, just as I suppose none of us do, at times. Sitting indoors now, the joy of "home" takes my breath away. Being "home" again seems surreal and takes my mind back to years ago when the proverbial "rug" of home was pulled out from under my feet. I had gone through a terrible time of sickness, of divorce and found myself full circle. Such is the circle of life - it forever goes round and we find ourselves in familiar places again and again - sometimes welcomed places and sometimes places we wish we did not have to revisit. Why then does the circle of life take us by such surprise? We know that the journey leads us round and round, yet still we seem stunned when we arrive at places we've been before. I suppose I was not just stunned but shocked when I came "full circle" those years ago.

I will never forget that last day when I packed up remaining belongings before turning in the key to my sweet little home. The weight of it fell heavy on me until it seemed as if my heart would burst. Instead of my heart exploding "I" exploded in a tirade of emotions - anger, hurt, loss, grief, fear - all wrapped up in a whirlwind of heated words. The look on my mother's face as those words came bursting out, along with the hurt in my heart I felt that day, seem forever etched in time. I was so angry! It had only been six and a half years since I had bought this home - "my home," the first and only one I had been able to acquire all on my own. It was a testimony of determination and perseverance... It was finally a place of refuge for my little boy and I after so much turmoil from divorce and hurt. We were happy! We were "home" and now we would soon be just boarders again in someone else's home. Sickness and a subsequent divorce had brought such financial hardship that I made the decision to sell. How could this happen? The day came and went and I dutifully went forward. My son Josh and I moved back in with my parents. It was humbling, consoling and exhausting.

Time moved forward as it has a way of doing - and much faster than I had realized. One night and several years later, I sat in my room at my parents' house and found myself lost in a sea of memories. As I looked around me, reminders of my past laid strewn like diamonds in the desert. Everything reminded me of someone from my past and those "someones" I was thinking of reminded me of "me" - the "me" I used to be from long,

long ago. I had felt so lost the past several years. Putting away freshly washed clothes in my closet, I saw a collection of decorative candy box hearts of various sizes - all of which had contained assortments of sweet delicacies from days gone by, now holding only memories. They were perhaps not unlike my own heart had been at times - a shadowy reminder of a full sweet heart. Several months prior, I had packed up a huge bag full of bears of every size, color and variety that inhabited this same closet. All of those "huggables," as well as the candy hearts, were tokens from the past. They, too, held bittersweet memories locked in their furry arms. It had been many years since I had kept a collection such as this. The previous one was packed away in storage somewhere like a time capsule. Having that most recent collection brought a simplicity that I had long forgotten. It had been an eternity since I had reached for a cuddly bear to snuggle up to during the night, but once again, I found that cradling one of them in my arms brought a comfort that I remembered from days gone by. Such a strange confession for a middle-aged woman, yet those painted expressions on the furry faces of my zoo critters hiding in the closet took me back. For a brief moment, things were not all that different from other phases of my life. I remembered the little girl who had the life-sized black and white Sylvester cat that followed me all the way to college. He had that permanent smile that brightened my day, he was a great listener and nice to cuddle with. Holding one of those cuddly "friends" as I would give way to sleep at night, softened the harshness of life… if but for a moment. They helped ease the confusion inside my head because I felt as if I had been catapulted through a black hole at warp speed ever since the day I shut the door for the last time to my little home those years ago.

It seemed as if I had always had a furry friend of some sort to bring me solace, comfort or simply to keep me company. At one point in time, the ivory bear wearing the lacey blue and ivory dress, with baby blue ribbons in her hair, sat staring at a young wife that I vaguely remember. That sweet bear offered a smile as I covered my own face with a similar painted on smile. That "smile" had masked years of pain from abuse, neglect and abandonment. What stories the little bear could tell if the lips of her smile were to open up and talk! Perhaps it was better that those lips were sealed... poor little bear. She had been packed and moved more times than I could count. Such was life living with an addict those ten long years. Always starting over, always trying to find a fresh start; running from the one thing that would always catch up with him - himself. That little bear was often joined by her "flesh and blood" brother of sorts, "Snowball" - my white Persian cat. He somehow knew when I was feeling low or sad. He would curl up in my lap and nudge my face and neck. There was so much being "said" in our silence.

As I continued to reminisce, I thought about the new mom who held a tiny stuffed brown puppy just inches tall next to my thirteen and a quarter inch, two pound and one ounce newborn preemie baby boy. I still recalled the night when I sat with that puppy in my arms, staring at cold sterile walls of hospital green, trying to find solace as tears stained my face. My sweet little brown-eyed boy had come much too soon as a result of the rages that had been unleashed on me by his father during pregnancy, but my little one was a fighter! He had held on for three more long months before his early arrival into the world. On one of the more difficult nights, I sat with a stuffed ball of fur wrapped in my arms, rocking back and forth as "Puppy" became a bundle of comfort for me. I was all alone that particular night in the parents' lounge, while the one person who was supposed to be by my side was not there. He was out on the streets somewhere nursing his hurts with his most recent "drug of choice." The loneliness was smothering, yet as I wrapped my own arms around myself with no one there to hold me, I sensed that someone had come into the room. There was no one - not another parent, nurse or doctor. Then, I felt an invisible set of arms holding us - "Puppy" and me. I wondered if that tiny baby sleeping in the next room would ever live to outgrow this furry brown stuffed friend of his. As I sat in the stillness of despair, I heard a familiar voice speak with a gentle whisper in my heart... *"You are not alone..."*

No matter how bad a day or night my miracle baby experienced, somehow I knew that he would survive and thrive because we truly were not alone at all. My little "angel" had angels watching over him day and night. Weeks turned into months and "Puppy" traveled a long way with my baby boy and I through long nights, lean days, and was forever a reminder of just how far we had come. He was eventually joined by the rainbow sherbet colored "Sunshine" bear who faithfully sang that sweet baby to sleep night after night. He never seemed to mind being wound up again and again as he sang... *"You are my sunshine, my only sunshine; you make me happy when skies are gray. You'll never know dear how much I love you..."*

As I continued to wade through the memories all around me that night in my parents' home, I noticed that the chest of drawers beside me displayed a crystal and brass dome clock that came all the way from Germany during my dad's time in the Air Force. Both the clock and I had been around the world and back, so it seemed. It reminded me of the coo coo clock Dad also brought back from overseas that hung on the paneled wall in our den when I was a girl. That clock was one of a kind. That crazy bird would "coo coo" thirteen times before he started his cycle over again. The cheval mirror at the edge of my bed just across from the chest of drawers was so much like the one I had in my home. I looked ever so carefully to see just a glimpse of that girl from so long ago. I sensed she was so close but still struggled with seeing her reflection again. In the corner behind me was a floor lamp. It had burned late many nights in my house that I still missed as much as I did those years ago when we sold it and moved out of our home. All these years, that lamp continued to burn ever so brightly, like a night star, reminding me that nothing was impossible and I should never give up no matter what. It was difficult to believe that it had been almost four years since such hardship had knocked on my door causing me to make one of the toughest decisions of my life. Being forced to sell my home was like slow death. A house may very well be only a possession, but a home is so much more. Our home was our safe place, our refuge; the heart from which everything in life flowed out from.

So there I was again, right back where I had started, so to speak, in my parents' home. Only this time, I was a parent myself and had my teenage son with me. Certainly a long way from the little girl back on Riverside Drive so many years ago. This was a not so welcomed reminder that sooner or later, we all come full circle in one way or the other. My time was much sooner than expected or desired. Where had the time gone? Where had "I" gone?

Some things never change though. I looked at the Bible on the nightstand next to my bed and remembered that familiar book that I had read since the tender age of nine. It was a book that I never strayed too far from no matter how full the "library of my life" had become. When I first read this divine masterpiece at such a young age, it was amazing that even a child could understand what its story was all about. It was ironic how simple the story seemed then and how complicated it had become over the years. My parents were very devout in their faith and beliefs so I was raised hearing the amazing stories of the Bible by the time I was old enough to talk. You could walk in most every room of their home (even the "powder room") and find a Bible ready to be opened in time of need. Not only did Mom and Dad read scripture to us as children, they prayed - about everything! I still recalled kneeling by my big old poster bed as a little girl. I saw my tiny frame, curly long brown locks, and big searching deep chocolate eyes. I was so small I could almost see under the bed when I knelt. It's funny. My prayer and my desires had not changed much over the years. I felt a million miles away from that little girl, yet strangely she was also as close as my heartbeat. In those bedtime prayers all she ever expressed was a desire to make God happy, her family happy and help others each day. She simply prayed that she would love others like they had loved her. I wondered. Had that come true at all? Did that little girl show that love really? Was she fulfilling her desires in life? Was she anything like she was meant to be? Sometimes I thought so, such as the day when my son and I talked about job prospects for him after he had graduated high school. I looked into the eyes of my then eighteen year old and saw the same fear and wonder I faced as I stepped out into life for the first time when I was his age. At that moment, I saw that this little girl did grow up to do something right. Looking deep into my son's eyes, for a brief moment, I saw my own heart - love poured out from a heart that love was poured into. He was so much a reflection of me. Yes, I could see that I had made a difference and done something right. At other times however, I reflected on my life and felt so lost. Who or what had I been since then? Who was I now? What was I becoming? I had traveled such a long road from our little neighborhood by the bay. *The curly-headed girl had skipped into the night, not realizing that it was a dark path into the abyss.*

That night sitting in my bedroom at Mom and Dad's, I found myself immersed in so many memories. I watched as my hands began to fly across the computer keyboard. I remembered the first time I sat at a typewriter in my high school typing class - an insecure fifteen year old, a naïve "church girl" who had so much to learn. It seemed ironic. There I was all those years later still tapping away at a keyboard without a clue. I felt so far away from that lovely teenage girl that was so full of inner beauty, yet somehow I sensed she was closer than I realized. The woman I was, had fallen so short of that "girl," at times. I had found myself in one of those "what now" moments, searching again for work like countless thousands in the present economy. Even with a good paying job before, I had to sell my home and depend on loved ones due to the devastation of divorce and illness. How hard it was to lose my independence that I had worked so diligently for! There I was at my worst, yet those who loved me stood right by my side. What was it exactly that they saw in me? What did I see in me? What did the God I totally believed in see in me? That Ancient Book with the heart stirring stories beckoned me again like a beacon in the night. In no time, the illuminating words stenciled across parchment pages began to shine into the deepest part of my being. Perhaps I understood after all. There I sat with absolutely nothing tangible to give or offer, feeling lost and yet possessing everything I needed. It was all tucked safely away inside my heart. It was of so much more value than the treasures I saw all around me that night. It was the same thing I had as that little nine year old girl. It was what caused me to "never give up," it was what caused my son to love his mom. It was what motivated elderly parents to stand by my side no matter how difficult the task. What was it? Something that I realized both the little girl and the woman protected at all costs - a purity of heart. Yes, I truly did have much to give and as long as "it" would beat inside me, "Starla" wasn't so far away after all. That night I embarked on a journey - one that began in my own heart.

CHAPTER 2

SEARCHING HIGH AND LOW

"...on a cold, foretelling December day, I walked down the aisle on my wedding day, slipped my hand out of my dad's and into the hand of a fate more frightful than I could've ever imagined."

This morning I woke with a memory of another summer day floating around in my head. It was a trip to one of the lighthouses here on the coast. I took a moment to pull up pictures from that day on my cell phone. It was a gorgeous day - clear blue skies, a brisk wind and a view of turquoise and blue Gulf waters that would rival exotic vacation spots all over the world. In this particular picture, we were leaning over the balcony that circles this quaint historical lighthouse. We captured a shot of our feet poking over the balcony's edge. Mine were totally bare! I had worn open-toed slides, which were not allowed, and was forced to leave my sandals at the base of the steps and tackle the hundred and ninety stair climb in my bare feet. As a sixties "baby," I felt a strange sense of belonging trekking up those winding stairs like a little "hippie." Strangely, I never felt more alive, more at home, more in touch with "me" in that brief span of time. When I reached the top, I felt such a sense of release. I danced in the warm summer sun and played an "air guitar" along with the music that the band was playing as they performed on the ground down below. All the cares that had weighed me down earlier that day were left behind. The pendulum of my life seemed at times to swing from high to low and low to high as quickly as the hands on a clock ticked forward. Balance was so hard to find no matter how hard I tried. The phrase "unhealthy relationship" was mild for what I had found myself in - again. This particular moment visiting the lighthouse was another high that I clung to for dear life because it had come on the heels of an excessive low and most likely would be followed by another one at the end of the day. My mindset was so conditioned that I had learned that I literally had to take things moment by moment because if I were to embrace the highs as part of the norm, the rug most assuredly would be pulled out from under my feet through some sort of tirade or another that would rob every moment of joy I had experienced that day. I was riding my life's "roller coaster" in another controlling, abusive relationship. My companion seemed to thrive on some sort of sadistic thrill in stealing the happy moments we managed to share with unspeakable moments of anger for no apparent reason. It had been fifteen years since I had suffered abuse from my first husband and though I couldn't begin to comprehend it, there I was in an abusive relationship again. It was too much for me to wrap my mind around. I had vowed long ago, after ten long years in a tumultuous marriage, to never allow such, yet I had naively jumped in one more time in an unhealthy relationship and there seemed to be no way out. Well on that beautiful afternoon at the lighthouse, for a split second in time, I was high above the world and all that it brings good and bad, if but for a moment. I was able to tiptoe through just a few minutes of life without a care. I thought of that old song *"Your love is lifting me higher than I've ever been lifted before..."* Love is a funny thing. It can lift you to the greatest heights and take you to the deepest valleys - all in the scope of a day, especially when guided by an insecure heart. I certainly had been to some of the highest "mountains" in the world, it seemed, and walked through some of the lowest valleys. It is such irony of circumstance that people who have been hurt deeply, love just as deeply. Lingering for awhile on this emotional "balcony" atop the lighthouse was a serene moment. Since that day, I had faced more of those "highs and lows" (all in the name of "love") so remembering a carefree moment where I was allowing my own heart freedom to dance and sing, was like a breath of fresh air. I had spent so many years nursing other wounded hearts, that I had numbed myself to the pain in my own heart. I suppose it was nothing less than a miracle how strong my heart remained. It was vulnerable but it certainly was not weak. I had always been such a loving, free spirit and no matter how many times I was knocked to my knees, I mustered hope eternal that love would always win no matter how many times "life" pushed me down. Some would say I was looking through "rose colored glasses." Perhaps I had been, but I chose to believe that I was simply looking through a telescope rather than a microscope. To me the glass was always half full. This acceptance of others had been both a curse and my saving grace. Perhaps if I had offered some of that same acceptance to myself I could have avoided some of my life's pitfalls. If I had learned the difference between accepting and enabling, some of those pitfalls might've never opened up before me in the first place. Yes, I was my own worst enemy, at times.

As I look again at this interesting moment captured in time on top of the lighthouse, I find myself a bit amazed that I was at peace with such a climb, especially with all the turmoil that was in my life at that time. Fear had become the norm and I was becoming more and more jaded regarding relationships. Perhaps there was something foretelling of my climb up to the top of the lighthouse that day. Looking back, I think it was another attempt to truly face fear square in the eye. Heights had always been one of my greatest phobias, my most visible battle with fear. It wasn't until my adulthood that I understood why. You see phobias, or perhaps the conquering of them, cause us to face things we are too afraid to face. Often the biggest fear we face is fear of ourselves. Sometimes it is hard to look at the face staring back at us in the mirror. While it should be the one window where unconditional love and acceptance shines through, often the mirror of our soul is our harshest critic because it reflects every emotion, every life experience, every secret thought, every action, every failure, every hurt, every pain, every hope, every dream, and yes even every success - all of them challenging and daunting in their own way. Some of us are so afraid of facing "self" that we live our lives in continual motion, lost in activity, because the silence in time alone forces us to face things that are difficult and downright painful; but ironically they never go away. At the end of the day when our head hits the pillow, all that we have run so hard from is still there waiting for us. I see now that this barefoot climb up those winding lighthouse stairs was my way of beginning to deal with the paralyzing fear that had gripped me again after so many years.

I still vividly remember facing my tall monster of fear the first time many years ago. I had made a life decision that impacted me and everyone around me in a way that would alter life forever. I gave my heart and pledged my life to a recovering alcoholic/addict. I gave my beautiful, pure heart to a man who had spent most of his life since adolescence on the wrong side of right, on the wrong side of the law and who had nothing to offer me even after I had given him ALL that I had to offer. He could barely protect himself from the claws of addiction, so caring for a wife was a daunting task. I had allowed him to step straight from the streets, through our church doors and into the corridors of my heart. It stills baffles my mind that this "good girl" could've veered so far from the familiar. There was something unsettling about southern girls. We seemed to be drawn to handsome mavericks of one sort or another. Who knows why? Many of us played out our role through a "Rhett Butler/Scarlett O'Hara" type attraction, so it seemed. I never dreamed that my search within would've taken me so far from home. I had allowed myself to fall behind in college partly due to ongoing health issues that had been with me since I was a young girl. I decided to come home with only seventeen credit hours left to complete for my degree. I was so very tired. It seemed that I stayed tired - emotionally and physically. This fatigue of heart and body had plagued me for so, so long. Perhaps it was sickness in my body or simply an aching in my heart. Who knows, but without the funds to go back to school another year, I had decided to finish my education at home. I allowed disappointment cause me to let my guard down after failing to reach my educational goal. I felt that I had fallen short. This was the true fear that seemed to plague me - falling way short of expectations, both mine and others. My self confidence was low and before I knew it, all those dreams of degree, career, relationship and family, were dashed by the unwise choice of a lonely, insecure heart. Ironically this choice was presented to me right inside church walls with no warning, no reserve. Our little church had embraced this man and supported him in the new life he professed since his "conversion." I embraced him as well without thinking twice about my decision. It was a fallacy somewhere in the teaching and mindset that a person "magically" changes overnight upon surrender to a higher power. Even the AA Twelve Step book talked about a daily change and courage to change as a journey not a one time process. I was not taught this, or perhaps I had been but had missed it somewhere, so my belief system opened up to this man with total confidence. I believed he was who he said he was simply because he had professed "faith." All I knew is that I had a heart yearning both to love and be loved and there seemed no greater way than to love someone who had been void of love for most of his life. How simple it all sounded then and how complicated it quickly became. If I had truly looked into the recesses of Daddy's eyes and listened to the pain in his voice the day we told him we were getting married, I might've chosen another path and life would've been much different for me. So much for hindsight. The truth is, I had a touch of a rebel's spirit so, most likely, I would've followed that path anyway. No one ever really saw that in me, ironically. This "Starla" could be compared to the little boy who had misbehaved and was told to sit in a chair in the corner for awhile. He would stand up only to be told *"sit back down."* Finally he could take it no longer and said *"I may be sitting down on the outside, but I am standing up on the inside."* I had always said and done just the right things in a feeble attempt at perfection that had been imposed on me always or perhaps that I had imposed on myself. Still, something in me had been standing up on the inside also - a restlessness, an unsettled spirit that poked hard at me.

So on a cold, foretelling December day, I walked down the aisle on my wedding day, slipped my hand out of my dad's and into the hand of a fate more frightful than I could've ever imagined. Eight years later, my life was in more turmoil than I could remember. What started out as a beautiful union of two hearts longing to experience love in its fullest and a desire to share that love through a life of helping others, slowly became a nightmare in the making. The reformed addict had stepped from the streets to a pulpit, and from a pulpit to a secret world I thought only existed in the movies. The desire to live out his second chance by offering that same chance to others, was being choked to death by hidden demons of addiction. What a web of secrecy he had woven around us both. I was literally hanging on by a thread in a multitude of ways. I felt as if I had fallen asleep in "Pleasantville" and awakened in "The Twilight Zone." In a last ditch effort to salvage marriage, life and sanity, I attended what was called "family week" for my spouse at a recovery retreat. The week was an emotional rollercoaster. Towards the end of the week we were faced with an outdoor challenge. With wisdom and insight, our counselors planned the day's challenges, increasing their level of difficulty as we went along. First was the familiar *"trust me and fall into my arms"* exercise; certainly more difficult than it appeared. Next, we were paired with another member of our group with a more challenging exercise in trust. One was blindfolded and the other was the designated mountain tour guide. Of course, I was chosen to be the trusting, faithful blind follower! Why not? I was already quite accustomed to that role with my husband. He and I had epitomized the concept of the "blind leading the blind." That day at this mountain retreat, my team partner and guide led me up and down hills and around steep curves. My heart was beating wildly and the heat was smothering. I felt trees, brush, and who knows what reaching out in an effort to stop me from invading their sanctuary. I sensed if I moved my feet an inch or more left or right I would experience a freefall down that mountainside. Finally, I was given the instruction to "*stop!*" I had quickly learned on this mountain trail that it was to my greatest advantage to yield to the instructions of my teammate. I put my feet in "park" and came to an abrupt halt. I removed my blindfold to find myself inches from a fast running river. How I wished there had been such a trusting "guide" in real life events. I had fallen off cliffs and stepped in over my head in the tide of life more times than I could count. Never really looking before I leaped, I had more zeal than courage, more willingness than wisdom and had often found myself on a freefall in the dark. I was hopeful that this river's edge was the climax to our lesson in trust. Soon however, our guide and counselor announced that there was one final challenge.

I had never heard of a "zip line," but once we approached its course, I was certain I did not like it at all! One by one, we were strapped down like a wild horse with a harness. We stood facing that same river at its lower edge. It ebbed and flowed, daunting and daring us to crossover. There was only one way - straight up. Halfway up that ten foot tree with my feet grabbing metal spikes like a vice, I realized I must've been completely out of my mind. None too soon, I made my way to a rope bridge that dangled across that river. Suddenly, the tree seemed like a fitting retreat; yet in this exercise there appeared to be no retreat. After what seemed like an eternity, my feet hit solid ground at the bridge's edge. Fear subsided, but only for a moment. Soon another tree was presented to us; this time thirty or more feet straight up. I approached this monster looming over me with its massive green branches waiting to wrap me up and swallow me whole. I felt like Dorothy did when she and the scarecrow were walking through the forest. We were not in "Kansas" any longer. My mind was spinning and my knees were weak. Firmly I grasped the tree, actually clutching it and holding on for dear life. I brought new meaning to "hug a tree!" Spike by spike, I climbed higher and higher as my spike "ladder" twisted and turned around this massive tower. Much like climbing the proverbial beanstalk, there was great uncertainty waiting at the top. A voice shouted faintly in the distance. *"If you don't want to or can't do this you can come down."* It was one of our counselors standing at the foot of the tree. Was he delirious from the heat? The thought of coming down was more paralyzing than the climb up. It had seemed like hours, but finally, FINALLY I was at the top! I grabbed the wood platform and pulled myself up with the help of the counselor waiting there. He clamped my harness to a large hook dangling from a heavy rope that swung high above us. I must've looked like a side of beef after the slaughter. The counselor took my hand and led me to the platform's edge and asked me to sit down. My feeble knees buckled. Sitting was good. *"Now take your time. You can do this,"* the counselor said. I looked out over the river that had threatened me moments before. It was still making a feeble attempt to taunt me, but this time it was more of a welcome call. All I wanted to do was put my feet safely on its other bank. A shout came from yet another counselor standing at the foot of this tall stage. It truly did seem like the scene from some "B" rated horror flick with fellow team members making their way up the tree beside me and others smiling deliriously on the ground across the river.

"How are you doing?" What a most absurd question. How in the world did he think I was doing? I was terrified! *"Okay now, tell me what you're afraid of?"* Again with the absurdities; he really had to ask what I was afraid of? I was thirty feet in the air dangling over the side of a platform, strapped to a rope that was tied across a swift flowing river with the rope being my only safe haven back to solid ground. Again he shouted, *"Starla tell me what you are feeling."* Much to my surprise, every fear I had ever faced came bursting out in a sea of exasperation. *"I am tired. I am tired of being afraid of everyone and everything. I am tired of feeling so alone and feeling as if I am just an afterthought. I am tired of the struggle. I am tired of trying to be perfect and feeling so afraid, alone and lost when I'm not. I AM NOT PERFECT and don't want to be perfect! I AM TIRED!"* The weights that I had felt as I sat down on the edge of that platform suddenly seemed more like wings. I truly felt chains breaking loose. I looked out through tearstained eyes at that river. It was flowing now almost like a peaceful stream. It wasn't so frightening after all.

"That's good to hear you say" the voice below shouted back. *"You know you don't have to be perfect, don't you?"* I had never known that before, but now it was a truth that illuminated my mind and heart like a candle in a dark room. I had never felt so empowered or so free. The little "church girl" didn't have to be perfect with everything she said and did. The addict's wife didn't have to be perfect and pretend everything was okay. She didn't have to hide behind the veil of ministry with her addict turned "preacher" husband who lived a double life. I didn't have to say all the right things or have all the answers. I no longer had to run, hide, or cover up the ugly truths that were stashed away like skeletons in a closet. I didn't have to feel that gnawing guilt of letting others down or disappointing those around me. I didn't have to do everything just right to earn their time or attention. I DIDN'T HAVE TO BE PERFECT! *"Okay now, when you are ready all you*

have to do is hold tight to the rope and slip off the edge." There was no time for thinking. It was now or never. Like an airline pilot, I was committed. I was at that point of no return. Before I knew what happened, I was plummeting across this river at what seemed like lightening speed on a downward spiral towards the other bank. As I came to a stop, I felt hands reaching up for me pulling me gently towards the ground. It seemed that an invisible set of hands were reaching down gently pulling my heart and soul to safety. I looked at my teammates. Those who had gone before me had ridiculous smiles plastered across their faces. Those who had yet to go still had that hollow look of fear in their eyes. *"How was it?"* Words could not describe what I felt. *"It was AWESOME!"* I couldn't believe the words coming out of my mouth. Was this the same girl who climbed that old tree in our backyard with her brother and neighborhood friends but was too afraid to swing down on the rope? I remember my brother Craig running to get help from Dad. *"Daddy, Starla's in the tree and we can't get her to come down!"* Now. here I was the older version of that little girl actually wanting to do the "zip line" again! Who would've ever thought that I would have to climb thirty feet in the air just to find myself?

CHAPTER 3

BROWN-EYED GIRL

"...despite the fact that she had the most amazing natural curly brown locks, adorable freckled face and piercing brown eyes, she had always been very insecure. Nothing she said or did ever seemed good enough. There always had to be more, more, more."

Recently, I picked up an order of contacts from my doctor. They truly are my eyes because without them or my glasses I am blind as a bat. I have to laugh at my "handicap" sometimes. Once when I was standing in front of a group and was speaking to someone specifically, two people could not tell which one I was looking at or talking to. I covered my right eye which is my worst eye, pointed at the person I was speaking to and said *"I'm talking to you."* Several years ago, my weak eye was damaged even more and actually crossed from a terrible time of illness. Focusing in on one person was quite a challenge. Whew! Sometimes I feel as if I am still "blind" so to speak, even with corrective lenses. There are moments like I encountered this week that absolutely leave me without a clue. I had faced yet another delay in my life that tested me to the limit. I kind of felt like I was that anxious woman again who sat on the edge of the platform ready to plummet across the river on the zip line. Except this time it was after dark so the "counselor" told me to sit and wait awhile!

Have you ever been in a situation where you feel you've done all you know to do, have done the right thing and still find yourself stumbling along your path in the dark? Sometimes, along our journey, the way is dark and just hard to see. We have to rely on more than our natural eyes to know the way. I had learned this lesson those years ago along the hike on my mountain retreat. Like that blindfold on me that day, "life" situations blindfolded me at times, leading up and down steep hills and winding trails as I held my breath wondering just how close to the edge I really was. Even those years later when I peered out at a beautiful world from a lighthouse high above my troubles, I still had not been able to see clearly. There had been so many moments in the "dark" - clueless it seems. Still, when the way was uncertain for me, I managed to put one foot in front of the other and move forward even with occasional "blind folds" on. I am not sure if it was blind faith or stupidity but at least I was not standing still! I suppose on some occasions it was debatable as to whether moving forward was the right thing or not; like the evening when I was leaving the house to go visit my friend Crystal. I "thought" I knew my path well enough to not turn on the porch light. What I had forgotten were our newest "family" members. Our cat had kittens and we had built a wood barricade to rein them in on the porch. I quickly remembered, however, as I barreled out the front door at full speed. My foot hit the boards and hurled me straight over the kitten's "den" with no brace to my fall. My knees hit the concrete flooring. Both elbows and palms slapped the floor. When I found my bearings, I regained my composure, stood up, limped down the steps and headed on to the car. I was too embarrassed to go back in the house for medical attention from my family. Once I arrived at Crystal's, all I could do was laugh between my moans. I had hit the concrete so hard that the green paint on the flooring had smudged off onto my white sweat jacket mixing with the blood from my scrapes! I was a mess.

This week's experience was another one of those "stumbling in the dark" days for me. I feel certain we all have them now and again. My sweet grandmother, Maw Maw Weeks has always tried to reassure me during these times. She is a devout Christian woman and totally believes that the Divine works in every situation in life. She would often tease us and say *"God may scare you to death but He is always on time and not a moment late."* Well if God is sitting on His throne looking down on me, He most assuredly has a smile spread across His face shaking His head at times… If He were "texting" His thoughts to me in this modern age, the keyboard would be worn out with "SMH" - "Shaking my head!" He might even speak to me in His best southern voice and say *"Bless your little heart"* which down South really means *"you don't have a clue do you?"* That would be absolutely true. Still, I am so happy that He loves this near sighted brown-eyed girl in spite of it all. I suppose being blind in many ways could be a blessing in disguise.

When I was only two, I decided that a toothbrush might be good for my eyes as well as my teeth and as a result, I severely damaged my right eye which required surgery that left me with only limited vision in that eye. It was quite a trauma for a toddler. I had scratched the cornea and was left with severe scar tissue and extremely blurred vision. For months, the least bit of light was like pouring salt in a wound. Eye drops, salves, daily bandage changes and eye patches became a bizarre and uncomfortable routine for a tiny little one. Though the injury healed, the vision never returned. Over the years, the strain on my "good" eye weakened it immensely also. When I was eight years old, my brother and I rode to school with our next door neighbor Matt. Each morning I would hop in the back seat behind his mother, Mrs. Lynch. Unfortunately, Mrs. Lynch was a chain smoker and I became the recipient of second handed smoke. The scar tissue in my damaged eye became infected and eventually required yet more surgery. I still remember it like it was yesterday. My eye was clamped open as I lay on my back on the surgical bed staring at a blinding circular light. Arms reached across me - back and forth; gloved hands grasping surgical instruments moved closer and closer to my face while I helplessly looked on. I could hear their voices and feel the pressure of them touching my eye but thankfully, no pain. Still, being strapped down was horrifying for a little girl. Once it was over and I was released, I was sent back home to start a familiar ritual that I had all but forgotten about as a toddler.

Vision impairment not only changed the way I saw the world, but how I "viewed" life and even myself. Seeing the world through blurred vision caused me to view those in my world with my heart instead of my eyes. I created a world all my own by what I "saw" inside. This is why I never really had a bad attitude towards others about what had happened. Oh, one could argue the "what if's" had I not sat behind Ms. Lynch each day riding to school, but the truth is, the damage had already been done and I had already spent six years since the initial accident with my "normal," so the recent setback was a bit easier to accept. As for Mrs. Lynch, she had no idea what had been happening to me. If she had, I am certain she would've taken care of the situation right away. Our families were very close. Back then, neighbors actually knew each other!

It's strange the little things you remember - like a yard full of golf balls after Matt and his parents had used our yard for their driving range. Dad would "pitch a fit," as they say in the South, every time he got out to cut grass. Or like the memory of seeing Matt's six foot eight frame through the den window as he passed through our breezeway to see if we could come out and play. He never could surprise us! As for his mom, what an interesting woman she was. I can still hear that robust laugh of hers. She enjoyed life, had an odd sense of humor and could cackle louder than anyone I knew - well except for my Paw Paw Weeks. Her favorite TV program was Charlie Brown. Whatever the season, my brother Craig and I would find our way over to the Lynch's den to watch the Peanuts gang for the holiday. Snoopy had met his match in Mrs. Lynch. She made the perfect co-pilot each time Snoopy came up against the Red Baron! The more Snoopy would laugh and snicker, the louder Mrs. Lynch would become. She, too, would howl! I must admit, those moments gathered around the television with the Lynch's were vastly different from what I was accustomed to. It was a rare occasion that our whole family sat together around the television in the evenings. Dad worked night shift for a few years and even when he was not on nights, those hands of my mother always had something to do, it seemed. There was often one chair empty in our family circle at night. Mom just could not sit still. She simply was not happy if she were not busy. My aunt told me once that my mother had been "grown" all her life. She had always been the little "doer." It took me many years to understand that this was her "love language." Doing for others was her true expression from the heart. As a young girl, however, I never could express to her how much we missed her during those ordinary moments - how much her daughter missed her. Those years that Daddy worked the night shift, Mom was too nervous to sit still. Being alone at night with two small children wore on her nerves so she stayed busy to occupy her mind. Even when Dad went on day shift and was home in the evenings, I could not honestly recall if she had ever laughed along with Snoopy. There were countless episodes of old programs like Gunsmoke and the Walton's that she missed with us. I am sure many reading this are too young to even know about these classic television programs, but they were a treasured part of our nightly ritual. Like the Walton's, we never failed to shout out *"Good night Starla, good night Craig, good night Daddy... Good night Mama. "*

As I began to heal after the second surgery on my eye, I started noticing changes in school. Our teachers usually assigned seats based on our last name, so I was always near the back of the room. I was a straight "A" student and would never dare think of being anything less, but I was struggling. It wasn't that I didn't understand the material; I just could not see the material on the chalkboard. Before long, I found myself attempting to read a chart on the office wall of my best friend's dad. He was an optometrist. Cindy and I had played in the back room of this office a million times modeling one fashion frame after another. I never dreamed I would ever actually have to wear a pair. What a world those little wire-rimmed glasses opened up for me. As we left the office that day, I realized something. I could read the road signs along the highway as my mom drove us home. The grass was greener; the sky was a vibrant blue. Who knows what I had been missing all these years. I was ecstatic. Yet with all I saw around me, I had not yet realized what I would see "in" me. When we got home, I anxiously looked in the mirror hoping to see something amazing there that I had been missing as well. I was not prepared for what I saw staring back at me. I desperately tried to be excited about my gold wire-rimmed glasses. After all, they had been the "in thing" since the Beatles. Something in me felt sad, however. I had no idea who that little girl was staring back at me in the mirror. She was a "girly girl" in every way, but *despite the fact that she had the most amazing natural curly brown locks, adorable freckled face and piercing brown eyes, she had always been very insecure. Nothing she said or did ever seemed good enough. There always had to be more, more, more.* Now, there was yet more… more to contend with than just making sure there were all "A's" on her report card, or that she was the top piano student, or wore her dresses just the right length, or said just the right thing, or was the perfect hostess to the neighborhood kids, or set an example for all the other children at church. Now she had to look at that plain looking little girl in the mirror and try to pretend she was happy with her. Perhaps she had been ugly all along and just couldn't see it. How I longed for that little girl again - that adorable petite little girl who would strut around in those white "go go" boots beside Cindy as she wore hers. *"These boots are made for walking, and that's just what I'll do, one of these days these boots are gonna walk all over you."* What a pair we were. Not now though. She was the cute one, this petite, blond-haired blue-eyed doll.

Tonight my heart feels sad for that little brown-eyed girl. She seemed so lost. How could anyone know what a simple pair of eyeglasses would symbolize for her? They were like mirrors to her soul - mirrors that she oftentimes was too afraid to look in. Even now, I am still mystified as to what that little girl was so afraid of. Perhaps I'll never know. For her, everything seemed okay looking through a cloud, but then came those glasses! She realized just how different she felt from other girls. For reasons unknown to her she was expected to be different - parents expected it, church members expected it, neighbors expected it and teachers expected it. She was weary of hearing how she should be the example for others to follow. It seemed like a huge request for such a tiny little girl. Well at least she was meeting expectations with these glasses. She was different all right. That pretty brown-eyed girl and her sweet smile seemed forever hidden behind wire-rimmed glasses.

CHAPTER 4

MEASURELESS MOMENTS

"It was the first time I had been without pain for as long as I could remember. I took a deep breath and digested the reverence of this moment. It was a moment that could not be understood nor measured by any human stretch of the imagination. It truly was divine."

A few years ago I sat in the State Employment Office looking across the desk of someone I had just met with a simple *"Have a seat. How are you today?"* Within moments, I began to form an idea of what this lady must be like. Behind her, there was a credenza cascaded with photos of various people in her life proudly displayed for all to see. Each one of them captured smiles of happy children and a proud mom - giving every indication that this employment specialist had lived a fulfilled life. One can only guess from what is seen in a picture, however. They say that a picture is worth a thousand words, yet sometimes, a snapshot speaks little to nothing of life's experiences. The momentary smiles captured mask a lifetime of emotion that one picture simply cannot express. I have album after album filled with photos of frozen smiles that speak little to nothing about a lifetime of emotions from one end of the spectrum to another. Sometimes a smile is a mirror reflecting the joy radiating from deep within one's heart, but at times it is a wall hiding pain and hurt deep within one's soul. It is often difficult to discern whether a smile speaks of measureless moments, or momentary masks. As my mind continues to be flooded with so many memories along my journey down "memory lane," I recall each life event with such clarity as though it is a "snapshot" or digital picture. Some of those memories are from childhood and of that sweet little brown-eyed girl so long ago, while others are more recent. Each of them are captured forever in my mind and heart in a way that cannot be tangibly measured. Every moment in life, good and bad, serves a purpose and makes a lifetime impression on us one way or another.

Recently, I watched a podcast where a speaker talked about being at the right place at the right time. His theory is that people cross our paths at just the right moment for purpose in our lives. It is so important that we recognize the value of moments in our day, seemingly insignificant events or daily encounters, and understand that they are so much more than chance - serendipity maybe, or better yet providence. A few minutes interaction can literally make a lifetime of difference; one small act or a few words can be life altering. Sometimes we may not even be aware of a moment's significance until many years later. One action or interaction or one decision can literally change a life or turn it in a different direction forever. My past is proof of that. One major decision by a young woman's pure heart, set me on a path of no return, taking me down a road I never dreamed I would travel. The lesson gained for me was that we must learn to listen to the whisper of our heart as to what to do with and in each moment. Our lives literally depend on it in many ways.

Sometime ago, I received a friend's request on Facebook from someone who had attended church with me for years. He was with me in the services, had engineered the sound booth when I sang. We had been crossing paths for eleven years in the same church and never met! Once he started communicating with me and we began to talk, I was surprised just how closely our lives had touched over the years. His mother lived on a street across the highway from my grandmother. When he was a little boy, his grandmother attended a church that my grandfather had founded and organized. Then, there he and I were in the same church, passing each other Sunday after Sunday. He had been right in front of me and I never knew it. When I asked my friend *"why"* we had not met, he teased me and said he had been *"admiring me from afar"* but it seemed I always had a man in my life so he never approached me. Of course it seemed to me that he always had women by his side too. We were more kindred in spirit than we realized - both seeking to fill an unexplainable void and battling a restless spirit within. In all honesty, I felt such sadness in my heart hearing him say this to me about the men in my life. He was right. I did always seem to have a man in my life - all too often the wrong man. In my adulthood, I had tried to make up for lonely moments that had troubled me as a young girl and teen. Ever since the day that I put on my glasses and had taken a good long look at myself in the mirror, I had experienced a loneliness that was hard to explain. Being able to "see" more clearly, caused me to lose sight of the little girl deep inside my heart. Still, loneliness seemed like a strange emotion given all that I had in my life. I had a good family, a lifetime network of wonderful friends, and had made many amazing memories with each of them, but still the loneliness poked hard at me some days. Even in a crowd, it would hover over me like a dark cloud. I had spent an eternity in dead end relationships so it seemed. What I had not realized, was that the loneliness would not subside just because I had someone in my life. Until one is comfortable with their own company, they aren't ready to truly enjoy or appreciate the company of others. I felt so ashamed of the number of past relationships - so much so, that I would battle self-worth when embarking on a new friendship. Through each relationship, I had exhausted every ounce of strength in me desperately trying to combat the emptiness within. Why do lonely hearts make such decisions? You can never outrun the one person you are uncomfortable with if that person is you! I had spent way too many years not seeing the "forest" because of all the "trees."

One Sunday, my new friend and I sat in church together as the choir presented the music. They began singing a familiar song to me… *"You are worthy oh Lord to receive… honor and praise."* The words were dancing in my heart and I began to sing them along with the choir. My friend had no idea, but his presence beside me was a gentle reminder of peace once again. I had all but given up on contentment. I had forgotten what it was like to feel so much serenity. I was having to re-learn how to relax, to feel safe and at ease in the moment because of the residual fear inside from my recent abusive relationship. Something told me it had been quite sometime since my friend had experienced this kind of bliss also. This was a moment that could not be tangibly measured but was of infinite value to me. The last three years of my life had been anything but normal or healthy, so experiencing a "normal" moment was like a gentle rain on a hot summer day to my parched heart. Later that day, we were chatting. I mentioned the choir song. I told him that I used to sing the solo portion of this song when I sang in the choir. I recounted the story.

Our choir had taken on the task of recording a CD. We recorded the choir portion during weekly sessions at the church and then had a live performance scheduled to mix in with our recordings. Each soloist had to schedule a time to go to the studio to record their songs for the CD. During this time of life, things were difficult for me. Actually "difficult" is an understatement. I had been battling a mysterious illness. What began as a migraine lasted sixteen months with no relief from the pain. I felt as if someone had a power drill driving it into my right temple. Daily my body became weaker and through test after test, the doctor's still did not have a clue. As time progressed, the nerves down the right side of my body began to atrophy and exhibit the same kind of stabbing pain. Although this recent encounter with illness and pain was different from anything I had ever known, it was not my first encounter with sickness. It seemed I had struggled with something my entire life. I was born pre-mature, and as I stated earlier - damaged an eye at two that required surgery then and more surgery at the age of eight. My freshman year of high school I was anemic, was always tired and would faint frequently; my sophomore year was spent running to the bathroom with an irritable bowel and vomiting. I had spent every year since I could remember with a headache of some sort - battling excruciating migraines; my college years I was so tired that the challenge of completing my classes due to chronic fatigue was insurmountable. Looking back, I think I must've been born tired. Following college, the trauma from an abusive marriage had only exasperated the fatigue and weariness my body felt. Now in my forties, I wasn't just tired, I was weary… totally exhausted from it all. All the things that I enjoyed became a chore - caring for my son, taking care of my home, working at my job, teaching classes or leading small groups and singing and playing the piano. Even hanging out with friends zapped my energy. These pleasures had become insurmountable tasks.

It was the final week allotted for soloists to record in the studio, and I had no choice but to try to get there and at least give it a shot. I was so weak I could not even drive. The final day for recording came, and I mustered all the strength I had to dress myself and have someone drive me across the bay to the studio. My head felt as if it were being pounded by a sledge hammer. My body was weak and I had dwindled down to a shell of what I had once been. I walked into the studio, desperately searching for the song in my heart. I meditated and prayed for strength. I needed help to get through this session. As I stepped into the sound booth, something no less than supernatural infused my body. The pain that had tormented me in my head, for over a year left just as mysteriously as it came. The music began to play and the words flowed from my lips with the sweetest melody. *"…You are worthy oh Lord to receive honor and praise."* With the last note, I sat for a moment and tears made their way down my cheeks. *It was the first time I had been without pain for as long as I could remember. I took a deep breath and digested the reverence of this moment. It was a moment that could not be understood nor measured by any human stretch of the imagination. It truly was divine.*

As I shared with my friend how I was the one on the CD singing this particular song, he shared with me how much our choir CD had meant to him. He had actually bought ten of them to give to family. The night that his grandmother was carried by the angels from this world, he and his family were playing this CD. Then again, when his uncle passed away, they had played our songs of worship. More recently, his stepdad had played the CD over and over daily. I had "been" with him and his family all these years - a part of some of the deepest moments in their lives. As we talked about this, I teased my friend and told him that I had been right there all those years and he didn't even know it, and also that he had been with me all those years that I stood in church singing this song and I hadn't even known it. In all seriousness, it was as if we had traveled through time and space touching each other's lives in moments that would only have meaning as time went on. Now years later, there we were sitting together in worship, his presence bringing serenity in that moment, just as I and our choir had brought comfort and peace to him over the years. People come in and out of our lives touching us in ways we often don't realize until we look back and see their fingerprints on our hearts. Sometimes we don't fully appreciate it until those moments are long gone and nothing but a memory.

Reminiscing about these moments frozen in time gives me courage on this journey of mine. I realize the importance of remembering key moments in life both good and bad. In times past, I had often been afraid of reliving those bad moments. However, even the bad moments are measureless once you look back and see what they've taught you, or the growth they have produced. Those moments must not be remembered with regret for that would only negate the lessons to be learned through them. What has seemed like chance or fate through each moment or encounter, has actually been divine providence. We can call it providence, fate, serendipity, but what I understand from this is that each experience, every encounter, the sum total of all my life's moments has led me to where I am and given me tools to get to where I am going. So, on days like today when I reminisce about days gone by, I search for the girl I was - that sweet little brown-eyed girl, look at the woman I am and reach out for the woman I desire to be, and in it all, I do remember. I remember bad times so that I stay grounded not to repeat the same mistakes, and also remember good times as those memories give me freedom and wings to fly. I must continue on this journey traveling to places I've been, stopping briefly where I am and charting a path forward.

CHAPTER 5

INSIDE OUT

"I don't know how, but I managed to flush all traces of the previous night's terror down the toilet. I felt sick and empty and ugly - and oh so alone. I wanted to run and hide but there was nowhere to go. Instead, I robotically made my way back to bed and cried myself to sleep."

Today I am thinking about a morning long ago. I opened the window blinds to face my day. It was another typical southern summer morning - a perfect scene actually. The golden sun was peeking down from a brilliant blue sky being ever so careful as not to wake the sleepy neighborhood too early on a Saturday morning. I suppose it is obvious by now that I love the South in the spring and summer time. That day is etched in my mind because it was another "epiphany" moment for me. Peering out that window that particular morning reminded me of something I had been feeling way too often. It was as if I had been on the outside of things looking in. That day as I stared out that window, however, I realized that it wasn't so much that I had felt like I was on the outside looking in but rather, on the inside looking out. On what? On a world and a life I longed for and knew was meant for me, but feeling trapped inside without a key or a clue how to get out. Somehow I think I am not the only person who has felt this way at times. We can become trapped in our own minds and ways of thinking before we realize it. It doesn't happen over night by any means.

When I was about eight years old, my cousin Ricky was visiting with us. Ricky is four years older than I and six years older than my little brother, so at the age of twelve he certainly was old enough to know about certain things. What can I say about Ricky? Even to this day, words do not adequately describe my dear cousin. If his older sister Cathy were reading this today, I would get a sincere *"amen"* from her. Ricky is one of a kind! He was a fun-loving, yet mischievous boy in a way you could not help but love. As his mom, my aunt Joyce might've said, he would *"aggravate the stew out of you"* - whatever that meant. (If you've never heard it, it is a southern term!) I tend to think it was Ricky that my aunt Joyce was praying for each night. When I would stay at their house I was always perplexed by the mumbling that went on after Aunt Joyce went to sleep. My aunt was, as they say in the South, "a praying woman," as was my mother, both my grandmothers and most all the women on both sides of the family. They prayed over the food, with their kids, for their husbands, before they went shopping and everything in between. Nothing was too small to pray about! Now you can believe it or not, but once my daddy was planning to climb up on the roof and repair it. Mom knew he was getting too feeble to do this kind of work, so she prayed. By seven a.m. the next morning a crew of men came knocking on the door. They said *"we were driving by and noticed that you had a patch on your roof that needed repairing. Do you need anyone to work on it?"* Well that was my Mom - her prayers had saved my stubborn daddy once again! But I digress. My aunt Joyce prayed each night in her sleep! I became so curious about her mumbling that I finally asked my cousin Cathy. Aunt Joyce was simply uttering - *"Jesus, Jesus, Jesus"* over and over in her sleep. It's no wonder with a boy like Ricky!

On this particular summer day when Ricky was visiting our house, he, my brother Craig and I were playing outside under the carport. I remember the days before the internet and Xbox when children actually played outside all day long. Imagination seems to be something of the past now replaced by its cheap counterfeit - fantasy. This carport of ours had become the backdrop for many adventures. It was a skating rink, a race track, a restaurant, a rock star stage, a stadium, a hospital. I honestly don't remember what our game of the day was, maybe hide-n-seek, perhaps cops and robbers or Cowboys and Indians; who knows. What I do know, by virtue of the fact that my little brother was the youngest, he was always given the least desired role in our game. Ricky, being the oldest and "wisest" came up with a perfect scenario for our little game. One thing I will say about him is that he was a clever little devil. No matter what we played, it seemed as though we really where there - China, the Old West, the moon or wherever our adventures took us on a day's journey. What fun we had! As our game progressed, trustingly, my little six year old brother found himself in a bind - literally. Ricky tied Craig up, gagged his mouth and put him in my dad's big toolbox! Perhaps he was the captured robber, or kidnapped Cowboy or Indian, I honesty do not recall, but Craig and I both played out the game without reluctance. I suppose I might've been concerned about my poor little brother, except for the fact that I looked up to Ricky and just like my brother, trusted Ricky completely. Ricky always took care of us and watched over us like a big brother. Craig crawled in that giant box, looked up at Ricky with those innocent puppy dog eyes of his and watched as Ricky shut the lid to the box. The two of us left the utility room and went back out into the carport to play. I can't begin to imagine what Ricky was thinking that day. It appears he wasn't thinking at all! I was no better than he. Our mindset that day reminds me of a quote I read recently by the king of cowboys himself, "The Duke" John Wayne. He stated, *"Life is tough, but it's tougher if you're stupid."* We certainly weren't the brightest bulbs in the pack that day! Soon, my mother realized that Craig was gone. *"Where is your little brother?"* I felt my heart sink. You can imagine the horror of this day. Let me just say Craig did NOT get over this experience quickly. I would suggest if you ever meet my brother that you not try to wrestle with him or hold him down and for heaven's sake do not ever get trapped in an elevator with him. What a horrible feeling to be trapped inside somewhere or something with no way out. After all these years, I think I understand what that little boy with the brown eyes as big as saucers must've been experiencing for those few moments he was trapped in that box - fear, anger, desperation and despair. I think I've always been gifted at making the most of difficult situations, and honestly have found my "back against the wall" more times than I can count. It's one thing to be up against a wall. At least you can pound on it to try to tear it down or perhaps attempt to crawl over it. You might even be able to find a way around it. You can even lean against it for awhile when fatigue sets in. It is quite another thing to be inside a place where there seems to be no way out. It's like being in a room with no doors or windows - smothering at times. I think it is because of the human need we all have to be in "control" that frustrates us during such moments. I often could not find a door or window in the walls of my heart because I had entombed myself with others' controlling behavior towards me and unrealistic expectations of me. Also, my lack of trust in my own actions and decisions created a life out of control. I had searched for that proverbial window or door for years.

I recall one night, in particular, when I found myself in one of those rooms of solitary confinement. I was living in another state far away from friends and family. The one person who should've been closest to me was a virtual stranger. He came and went, came and went and I never knew who or what he would be when he did return. My first husband the addict/preacher/business man/drunk was out of control. I still loved him with all my heart just as I did when I first married him. He was the first man I had given myself to and opened myself up totally to, but he had become a stranger to me. I so longed to have my husband back - that man that had made my heart smile and knees weak in the beginning. In those last several years of our lives as his addiction became full blown, he was still trying to hide his secret life from family, from friends, from church acquaintances and from our clergy associates... and to some degree from me. The night had been literal hell for me. He had not returned home from work, had not called and I had no way of knowing where he was or even how to contact him. For hours on end I paced the floor, looked out the window, prayed, cried then fumed, then shook from fear. Eventually, I called hospitals just in case he had been hurt, but there was no trace of him. He was nowhere to be found. Sometime in the wee hours of the morning, I drifted off to sleep from sheer exhaustion. With daylight, I heard the slow turning of a key in the lock. Finally, he was home. I did not recognize the man standing in front of me - literally. My husband "said" he had been in an accident and passed out from the blow in his truck on a remote street. He had been in an "accident" all right, but it was not due to an automobile wreck. No, it was from a life that was wrecked in the worst way possible. His face had been beaten to a pulp until he could barely open his black and blue eyes. His lip was turned inside out and his face etched with gashes. I pleaded with him to go to the hospital. He refused. I questioned him over and over about the truth and he would not budge on his story. I was so sick I could not stand. The room was spinning. I managed to clean his wounds with a wet cloth, then he made his way to the bedroom and fell across the bed for some sleep. I tried to lie next to him, hoping it would bring comfort, but all it did was smother me. I felt like a prisoner in my own home, my own life. As the hours passed, I began cramping. It was a physical reflection of the deep emotional gnawing inside my heart and soul. I made my way to the bathroom. I had not even told my husband, but I felt that I might be pregnant. Soon it was evident. What had been a life was no more. *I don't know how, but I managed to flush all traces of the previous night's terror down the toilet. I felt sick and empty and ugly - and oh so alone. I wanted to run and hide but there was nowhere to go. Instead, I robotically made my way back to bed and cried myself to sleep.* I was so ashamed of it all that I never even went to the hospital. What could they do for me? It was too late - too late for anything it seemed... Shame had become my way of life. I had spent years covering and hiding under the pretense of love and protection for my husband, for the ministry, for "God" not realizing that there was a world of difference between love and enabling. Love was not weak, but I was, and the longer the charade went on, the weaker I became - mentally, physically, emotionally and spiritually. I was a shell of who I had once been and no longer living - simply existing in a dark world of fear, loneliness and pain. I felt so alone. My husband's world took him to a place far apart from his life with me, and when he was home, he was there but not really "there." It seemed, at times, that I was all but invisible. He was my world. How I longed to be his again. I was so jaded from seeing the dark side of life that holding on to my faith was a monumental task. How could a "man of God" exhibit such disregard for others, for God, for himself? I knew deep down that he loved me and loved God, but a stronger force than his weak will was in control. Addiction was his mistress and he was at her beckon call. How could I allow so much to go on, keeping silent knowing that others were being deceived and hurt? Fear had become my master. Why hadn't God stopped it? Stopped him? Delivered me? I was in such a dark place, that I simply could not see the light of God's love that was trying to pierce the deepest dungeon of my soul. I tried to make it all right for my husband, for my family, for those we worked with in ministry, but I was so lost and afraid; the shadowy place I had found myself in was entombing me until little by little, the very life was being sucked out of me. My young baby's life was not the only "life" that was flushed away that day. Thinking of all of this then and now I realize just how long I had allowed myself to feel like a visitor in my own life - longing for a door to walk through that would lead home. Through it all, I kept just a small measure of hope that this invisible door was closer than I knew.

Days after this event, I felt as if I were being shut in - totally smothered. There was nowhere to go, no door to step through or window to open that I could fly away from. I lay in the floor of my beautiful new home and caressed each possession with my eyes to try and find solace, tenderness, peace, but nothing - absolutely nothing would calm the storm deep inside. I pulled at my long curly brown hair; I wrapped my skinny arms around my own body and rocked myself like a baby much like I did those years later in the neo-natal unit of the hospital when my son was born. Tears fell from my hollow deep brown eyes burning my pale cheeks. *"God I can't deal with this anymore. I would rather not live if this is how life is meant to be for me."* Now whether it was literal or in my mind's eye, I can't really tell you, but the gentlest man I've ever seen walked into the room. He was tall with fair skin, light reddish-blonde hair and had kind, sparkling eyes that looked into my very soul. I felt as if he knew me, he understood me even when I didn't understand myself. He wrapped his arms around me where mine had just been and spoke just a few simple words... *"Everything is going to be all right. You are loved and you must believe that you are not alone and the day will come when you won't ever have to worry about being alone, afraid or hurt again... don't give up."* Just as quickly as my "angel" came - he left. Through all these years, I never forgot his words or his smile. On days when my strength would wane or my hope wore thin, I would remember his face, I would hear his words and I never stopped walking forward and believing the words divinely spoken to me. On days when all was dark and I really couldn't see the path clearly in front of me, I knew that if I continued to listen to that sweet and loving voice inside my heart, somehow I would find my way home.

CHAPTER 6

THE STAGE OF LIFE

"For years I wore a mask hiding all the darkness in my life. When people saw me, they saw a smile on my face. When I spoke with them on the phone, I made sure there was a 'song' in my voice."

What a strange new world we live in. Everything is about instant communication. Several years ago when I was looking for work, I received a text message on my cell phone from someone named "Kim" at an employment agency. She supposedly had a job opening in my area "just for me." All I had to do was go online and register with their jobsite to apply for the job. She had not seen or talked to me, but was interested in hiring me for a job. How could she possibly know if I would be a good fit or even qualified for the position? Do people even talk anymore? Do they truly see each other anymore? I read a story sometime ago that discussed the impersonal nature of group meetings. The example was quarterly sessions for school teachers. They had "virtual" conferences and training sessions online. While these online conferences are not new and most every business venue operates within these forums, what is interesting is how the teachers in this particular forum interacted with each other - under an assumed identity. Each teacher could choose an "avatar" that represented who they wanted to be. You can make this virtual "person" look anyway you want - tall, skinny, long hair, short hair, blonde, brunette, muscular, handsome, beautiful etc. No one ever has to know the real you. This is common in the gaming community, but seemed a bit odd for business colleagues. More recently, I joined an online contest that required daily interaction through a similar forum where we posted progress. We, too, had the choice of posting a picture of ourselves or choosing an "avatar." One lady, in particular, posted a picture of "herself" at the beginning of the contest. She was an African American. Later, she was of Asian nationality and then finally she posted what we think is her true picture; she is a fair skinned blonde American woman! We are forever wearing a mask aren't we? It seems so interesting that everyone in the contest has bonded and become close during the process of the online competition. Yet, no one has met the other face to face, or for that matter knows one another in real life. The truth is, it is a stage where we have a choice of being our true authentic selves or if we choose, we can simply project a persona of only what we want others to know. While I love the interaction of social forums, I feel something is truly lost these days in human relationships. Life is a stage, so it seems. We are always performing for others in one way or another. Peer pressure seems to be greater than ever no matter what age a person is. So many people are living duplicitous lives afraid for certain people to truly know who they are. They live one life at church, synagogue, temple or community, at school or in their neighborhood, another one at work, and another one with certain friends or family. There is such a fear of rejection, that often people just can't find the courage to be vulnerable and transparent so they have a closet full of masks for every occasion. I confess… I've certainly been one of those people with a fear of rejection, at times. I struggled with it as a child. I gained much understanding as a young college woman and began to conquer it to some degree, but then the secret world I lived in for over ten years with my husband's battle with addiction, fed that monster of fear. I've worn my own masks in many situations - even with those closest to me. Ironically though, we can only wear those masks for so long. I learned this hard lesson trying to maintain a measure of normalcy in the outreach with my husband despite his duplicitous lifestyle. Once I found the courage to allow others a glimpse inside my heart and life, I discovered something so liberating. Love stands with arms of acceptance. We don't have to hide or be afraid. I am slowly learning the art of transparency. The greatest acceptance one finds through transparency is acceptance of self.

For years I wore a mask hiding all the darkness in my life. When people saw me, they saw a smile on my face. When I spoke with them on the phone, I made sure there was a "song" in my voice. We can become quite proficient at hiding can we not? I had worn my façade for so many years. I am not certain why, but I just felt if others knew the truth about the deepest pains in my life, about my tumultuous marriage, the abuse and everything in between, that I would appear to be a dismal failure. For them to know that I was staying in a marriage partly due to fear was even worse. What would they think of me? How weak I would appear to them. I had been rejected so many times by my own husband who was supposed to love me more than life; I could only imagine the rejection I would experience from family and friends. How distorted my thinking had become. I had never truly overcome that insecurity that had haunted me my whole life - that feeling that whatever I did was never enough. How could I possibly tell my family and my friends that my marriage was so rocky? That my husband was not the perfect spouse? That my positive outlook had done nothing to improve my life? That my faith was not producing the results I had prayed for? I longed for someone to just believe in me and see ME without all the "stuff" and tell me it was okay - I was okay. We never stop that quest for affirmation and approval do we? Life is forever a stage. Even in current relationships, sometimes I find myself slipping into this protective mode of performing and fearful of being real. We often send pictures and text messages instead of talking. It is easy and safe, but it robs us of truly touching. Even if it is the newest wave in communication, it steals away intimacy and closeness. Some time ago, I asked someone close to me why they would not simply pick up the phone to talk to me when we were trying to resolve a conflict. Their response? *"I suppose it was just easier to read your disappointment rather than hear it in your voice."* It is ever a struggle to not be up on that stage.

I still remember one of my first stage experiences at the ripe old age of nine. It was my first singing encounter. Cindy, Lisa and I had the perfect trio. We were destined for greatness. We had the perfect song to sing during that Wednesday evening youth service. Our song even had three verses! After Ms. Naomi gave the piano introduction, off we went. My best friend Cindy stood clutching her pretty lace dress twirling each end with her hands. If the song had been too long, she would've had that dress in a total knot! Cindy's cousin Lisa was the envy of all the other girls, (at least in her mother's heart). It was no surprise that she stood with perfection, belting out every note and remembering every line with amazing clarity. As for me, I tried my best to overcome the fears and remember what my mom, the choir director had taught me. *"Just look past the crowd to the back of the building and focus on something. You will be less nervous."* So much for trying, however. My eyes never made it past the front row where my little brother Craig and his friend Jimmy sat. It seems it had become their mission to totally sabotage our first public appearance. Those mischievous boys made every face a little boy knows how to make. All my composure left, and laughter escaped through those singing lips pushing melody totally off stage. It is true what they say, *"laughter is contagious."* Cindy began laughing as well, and then finally the whole crowd burst into laughter; everyone, that is, except for Lisa. She knew better. Her mother would be quite upset if she did not perform perfectly. That cute little black-haired girl sang three verses solo with laughter as her accompaniment! That was the longest five minutes of my life. We exited the side stage and ran outside the church to slip in the back door. I vowed to never put my foot on a stage again! Forty plus years later, I recall scores of recitals, singing events, church services, conferences and more times than I can count where I said *"never again!"*

We spend so much time beating ourselves up for this insatiable need for approval. What we don't realize is that it is the way we were designed and are wired. If you are a church attendee what are you doing each week as you participate in a church service? You are offering praise and affirmation to God. Yet we struggle with desiring that for ourselves? Why should we be so ashamed of the fact that we need praise and affirmation? We spend huge amounts of money and invest a tremendous amount of time into celebrities and athletes who make a living off of receiving praise and affirmation and seeking approval. Why do we struggle in our personal world with that need? From the time children are old enough to walk and talk, they become involved in various hobbies or interests - all of which allows them the chance to step up on one stage or another so that they can shine and receive praise and approval. Little ballerinas on tiny tippy toes, toddlers in tiaras, tough tots playing tee-ball, soccer sons jutting across a field, football fanatics aiming for a goal post, musical maestros creating magical melodies… all on a stage seeking affirmation. I believe that there are two things that everyone needs - hope or something to look forward to, and value - someone to believe in us so that we in turn can believe in ourselves. We step out on this stage of life early on like actors in a play hoping to please our "crowd," our family, our friends, our schoolmates, our parents; then our companions, our kids, our bosses or even the stranger in the grocery store. Life seems to be nothing more than a room full of mirrors where our image is constantly changing based on where we are and what we are looking at. People see us the way we want them to see us. It is no wonder that we lose sight of ourselves along the way sometimes. Even now through all the lessons I've learned, it is still a challenge not to be on that stage, but my heart's desire is to be real and vulnerable and unafraid. It is easier said than done after so much hurt, betrayal and loss of trust - but it is all the more necessary. I want to be authentic more than anything. I must find the courage deep inside of me at all costs if I truly value my relationships and friendships. I must be okay with the fact that I have no great story to tell, no feats to boast of. I must move beyond feeling ashamed to tell those close to me about all the difficulty life has brought my way and yes, even how I have stumbled and fallen at times. While it is certain that the "truth will set you free," it takes courage to walk in truth. Courage - it is not the absence of fear, but simply resolve and determination to face that fear even if I am "shaking in my boots," so to speak. Still, sometimes questions bombard me like the spray of a shotgun. What will they think? Will they draw near or shy away? I want approval, just as we all do. I long to know - really know that my friends and loved ones understand. After all these years, I am still learning the lesson that true love and true friendship accepts and understands and is not based on conditions. Years of abuse and blame for things I did not cause, damaged my perception considerably. I can conceive the concept of acceptance mentally, but sometimes emotionally deep in my heart, fear casts dark shadows on the light of love's precious truths. That fear of rejection still clouds my heart every once in awhile.

As I come face to face with my own fears, I have begun to realize that all of us have things we hold deep within with fear and apprehension, and often denial even. I suppose we only tell our stories in part. We sometimes use smoke screens and mirrors to hide the deep part of our heart that we are too afraid to face. Life sometimes leaves scars. Often, we divert by hurting back or pushing the very ones away that we desire in our lives, in order to numb our own pain. Another confession - I've done this very thing. I did this several years ago during the second abusive relationship I found myself trapped in. I was too ashamed to reveal the truth to my family, my son and my friends. I tried every way I knew and used every smoke screen and mirror in my "magic kit" to convince everyone how wonderful this man was - how amazing our relationship was developing. As time went on, I found myself spiraling down a long dark tunnel headfirst with no safety net. At some point, the fear I felt for myself was replaced by fear for my family, so I pulled away from them all. I disappeared weekend after weekend, holiday after holiday. My son spent many lonely hours without the one person who had always been his constant. The more I hurt, the more I hurt those I love even though I tried so desperately not to. One day something snapped in me. The whole ordeal played like slow motion before my eyes. The pain on my son's face and the desperation in his voice slapped me back into reality. Like so many years before when I had walked away from his father, I found a courage that had been long lost, and I walked away one more time from one more perpetrator of pain and hurt. Something in me knew that this man was hurting me because of the unspeakable hurt he had endured as a child, but I still could not allow my compassion to cloud my judgment. No one has the right to harm another human being - not physically, mentally or emotionally. Recently, someone I care about very much pulled away from me like I did my family so long ago. How hard it is to be isolated from someone we long to lavish love on! Feeling this myself causes me to grieve because of the hurt I've inflicted on others in the past. Hurt breeds hurt, and sometimes, we sabotage our own happiness because we can't seem to let go of our hurt not realizing it is only a shadow from the past rather than a roadblock in the present. It isn't until we experience unconditional love, that we fully understand this shadow that hurt casts over our lives. This is what my son showed me even when I was so hurtful by shying away from him. When another person shows such a depth of love for us, it opens up our own hearts so we can begin to love ourselves as we should. Each of us just wants to be loved, not for what we have been or done or are or will be, but just because. We simply want to be accepted - plain and simple. Even in adulthood, I have found myself "on stage," so to speak. Not with my brother and his friend sabotaging me from the crowd, but mistakes, painful mistakes from the past taunting me. They have been difficult to forget or wipe away. It has not been a friendly crowd laughing with me, but a cruel world laughing at me. At least that is the way the enemy of my mind would have me feel. I have heard hurtful words from my past ringing in my ears sometimes. Words like *"you've never had anything, been anything and never will."* Other words like *"what man would want you, you have nothing left to offer?"* People can be so cruel at times. My mind has known that those were just words from other wounded hearts, but my heart has struggled. Yes sometimes, I still struggle with simply desiring to step off the stage and never "sing" again. Fear, disappointment, failure, betrayal and hurt can alter a person's ability to open up. What I have begun to realize is that I have not fully allowed others to see "me" because I myself have struggled with the courage to see "me." No one really wants to face their hurting, fearful side. Something quite amazing has begun to stir in me, though. Love and acceptance from those who mean the most to me has poured into my hurting fearful heart like a medicine. I have found the strength to open up again little by little. I have begun to see some of the very things in others that have been hidden in my own heart. Peering into their souls through eyes of love has been like my own reflection in the mirror. What have I learned in all of this and what do I see now in that mirror? I see a woman who has found courage to look at herself - scars and all and to see beauty there in spite of them. I see beauty in the ones I choose to open up to beyond their scars, their fears and their failures. Each time I find myself pulling away from others, I remember my mother's words after that premier performance so long ago. *"You have to get back up there. Everyone's afraid. I am every Sunday when I step on that stage. Everyone messes up sometimes. It's okay, but it is important to try again."* The voices are different, but the words are the same. Even though they aren't spoken, I "hear" them in a smile or outstretched hand from a friend or a loved one, and with those small gestures of love and acceptance, I get back up one more time. As I do, I learn more about not just reaching out for a hand but extending a hand in exchange. Acceptance is a two-way street.

CHAPTER 7

THE SOUND OF MUSIC

"So many things had tried to silence the song in my heart, disrupt the harmony of my life and drown out the melody within my spirit. Illness tried to muffle it, abuse attempted to stifle it, critics desired to steal it and failure wanted to silence it."

From as early as I can recall, music has always been a part of my life. My mom was a choir director, my uncle was a choir director, my cousin was a choir director; my grandmother, aunts, uncles, cousins, brother and mother to some degree either play the piano or sing. In more recent years, two of my younger cousins have become songwriters both producing and recording music and traveling. So quite naturally, I began singing at an early age. I began taking piano lessons when I was only nine years old - right after I began wearing glasses and adjusted through my vision issues. There was always the sound of music somewhere around our house or with our family. Holidays were not complete without someone sitting at the piano and a group gathering around singing carols, or hymns or whatever the special day demanded. We would sing in the shower, sing in the car, sing at church - on stage or in the pew, sing in our room, sing on trips and sometimes sing in our sleep. We were always singing! Although I loved singing, I soon learned that my forte' was actually playing the piano. From the first few lessons, I took to the keyboard like a duck to water and fell in love with the whole experience. I learned rapidly, and found that there was a world all my own in those ivory keys. I could get lost in my music if only for a little while. It was there that the shy girl found safe haven - I was home. It was my way to be fully expressive without intimidation. By the time I was twelve, I was playing the piano for the mid-week service at our church. By the time I was sixteen, I was "the" church pianist. After I overcame my first stage appearance that night with my little friends, I soon rid myself of the fear, and performing on stage became a weekly activity for me. My instructors were delighted at my enthusiasm and how quickly I caught on and how I grasped theory concepts beyond my years. By the time I was in the seventh grade, I was doing twelfth grade music theory and performing pieces that others were tackling in college.

Sitting on a piano stool was one of those places I truly felt important, accepted. It was there that the pretty popular girls were no match for me. It was there that my family was proud of me. It was there that a shy insecure girl was somebody. For a moment at least, the music drowned out the voices in my head. The cheerleaders, gymnasts, jocks and what I deemed as "cool" people had to take a back seat. I fit in with the brainy nerds much easier. Yes, I had found my "place" resting on that piano stool, with my hands strolling up and down the ivories with precision and grace. When I was in my teens, I decided to compete in a teen talent competition. My piano teacher was absolutely the best in the city. She had begun playing at the age of three and advanced at an unbelievable rate and measure. Pam was the woman that everyone called on to play at their wedding, to accompany mass choirs at major events and the one who had the long waiting list of students that would stay on the list for months just for a chance to become a student of hers. Pam helped me create a unique piece for the competition. It was an interesting and exciting compilation of contemporary and traditional songs, showcasing my versatility and style. Rounds one and two, the local and regional competitions went off without a hitch and were a cinch. I was under no delusion, however, that the state competition would be the same, as I knew the best of the best from all over the state would be there representing their regions. The competition did not separate the contestants by age, so there would be young people from age thirteen all the way to age nineteen. It didn't really seem fair that a junior high student had to compete against a freshman college student, but it was a teen competition and all was fair game.

The day of the event was a hot summer day and the competition was being held in an open air tabernacle type building in north Alabama. It was summer in the South and we were competing in an open building with no air conditioning! I was so nervous I could not breathe. The heat did little to help. The day seemed eternal. There were various talent events from solo singing to brass ensembles, from choirs to drama teams and from creative writing to percussion. Finally, the day would end with the piano competition. I had tried all day to stay focused and to keep my mind on my performance piece. It was quite long and complex, and all of the day's events could've served as serious distractions. I found moments in between competitions where I was able to sneak a few minutes to work through some of my piece on the piano when no one was in the auditorium. I don't recall how far into our portion of the competition I was - maybe fourth or fifth, but finally my name was called! All the adrenalin rushed to my head, I took a deep breath, stretched my fingers, sat silently for a moment to gather my focus and then began my stroll across that familiar path. The black and white keys welcomed me. The music ebbed and flowed, loud and soft, fast and slow and then… the end. I felt confident in what I had done that day, that is, until "he" sat down. I knew "his" performance was coming, but had tried to push it out of my mind. I would've never been able to maintain my composure otherwise. He was not a boy at all, and was still a teen only by a few months. Actually, he was nineteen and in college! He was a music major, nonetheless. To make matters worse, he was performing a piece he had performed at the competition a year ago. He had been given plenty of time to perfect his piece. Here I was a shy insecure young high school girl with a relatively new piece, competing against a seasoned college "man!" After the final note, the judges were dismissed to compile the scores and make a decision. Whatever the outcome, at least now we could all relax.

The awards announcement ceremony got underway. Category winner after category winner was announced. Some went forward to receive their trophies, others ribbons. Last again was the keyboard competition results. At this point, I had no clue where I would rank. One thing was for certain, it would not be number one. Tension built as each person was ranked and then came the finale'. *"First runner up for the state is… Starla Rich!"* I knew what was coming next. Of course the college boy won. But ironically, I was ecstatic! Little insecure Starla, that freckled face school girl was first runner up to the "college man!" It wasn't often that I felt the way I did that day, but it was a feeling I have never forgotten, then or now. No one had given me that moment. I earned it and no one had the power to take it away from me. I had given my all. I felt such an amazing moment of empowerment and acceptance. My self-worth skyrocketed. For that moment I had lived up to my name. The affirmation felt wonderful. This competition set the stage for other competitions culminating with a music scholarship for college. The sound of music found its way from my home near the sandy white Gulf Coast beaches to a college dorm in the plush mountains of Tennessee. The sound of music resounded across time and space from childhood to womanhood. Music was the one thing that soothed the flaming insecurities deep in my heart.

Through some of those years through adulthood, I had allowed that sound to become silent. Life had become so loud that the song was barely audible - not literally, but figuratively in my heart and soul. Actually, there was a period of my life that I could not even bring myself to step up on a stage to sing. I did continue to play the piano, but each time I sat down and began to run my hands up and down the ivories, I felt a rage inside. It was compulsory performance, not a gift of expression from my heart. I was participating with my husband in his ministry and public speaking endeavors while trying to hide the horror that had become our lives in secret. He was so bound in his secret addiction and I was fearfully devoted. I wanted the song to come forth, but it would not. Each time I tried to sing, my mouth was like cotton and fear gripped me like a vice. It was so hard to understand because I had been performing since I was a small child and rarely felt fear. This was simply a manifestation of the terror that had become my daily life. When I played the piano, I tried very hard not to cast a hurtful glare at the man on stage. I had allowed him to steal my song. Finally, the day came when I found the courage to come off the road. I acquired a full-time job and he traveled the highways alone. He wanted to believe he was so self-sufficient, but obviously that wasn't the case because things quickly fell apart and soon, he came off the road also. I knew deep inside how desperately he needed me by his side, but he could not face his own weaknesses, which is the very reason he stayed swimming in a sea of addiction and living in a dark world of chance - playing Russian Roulette with our lives.

I can't honestly say exactly when I felt the song die in me or even when I felt a rebirth, but somehow the gentle melody of hope began to resound in me. *So many things had tried to silence the song in my heart, disrupt the harmony of my life and drown out the melody within my spirit. Illness tried to muffle it, abuse attempted to stifle it, critics desired to steal it and failure wanted to silence it.* Thankfully however, love drowned out the noise of the world and dialog from the past with a new song. It took much time and patience to turn me around from clouded thinking, but patience and kindness towards me opened my eyes and heart. In times of meditation, I was reminded ever so tenderly that it wasn't about what others did or didn't do, or what I did or didn't do, it was all about God's divine love. Once again, the sound of music filled my heart. One evening I had stopped by my church at the end of a dinner date. I had been working as the music assistant so I had a key to the facilities. This was a special place for me, a place where I had allowed the sound of music flow into my heart and then to resonate out to others. This was a sacred refuge for me. That evening, I slipped in, turned on the lights in the hallways and my dinner companion stopped off by the restroom. I then slipped into the sanctuary and set the lights to a soft, reverent glow. It had been a while, but I sat at the piano. As soon as my fingers touched the ivories, that new song from recent years began to flow from my heart through my hands like a fountain of life. I confess, I had played that song untold times, but at times it had only been notes across piano keys, not a song from deep inside. This night however, the melody was much more than ritual. I embraced that familiar feeling as it touched every area of my soul. I was unaware, but my friend had slipped in to listen. He sat there reverently quiet, digesting this sound of music into his own heart and soul. In all the time he had known me he never knew that music was a part of my life. As he listened, the sound of music filled the air resounding from the recesses of my heart. There was a sweet sound of harmony between me and divine love that permeated the air. This was a song poured out of my grateful heart. It was the same sound of music from days gone by that was leading me full circle as it played deep within. I had followed the deceptive tone of the pied piper for too long, so this tune was ever so sweet to my senses. I tuned my ear to listen to this welcoming song and determined in my heart to try to dance to its rhythm regardless of what life brought my way.

CHAPTER 8

LAYER AFTER LAYER

"Instead of trying to escape his abuse, I cried silently into the night until exhaustion gave way to sleep... I feel exposed today. That trauma was so many years go, yet scars that I thought no longer existed still remain.... I have covered them with emotional 'shirts and sweaters'... trying desperately to look beautiful, to feel beautiful and to be okay."

Today is Good Friday and the impact of what this day truly means has weighed heavy on me. Being a part of the Christian faith, this is a Holy Day for me. We remember the crucifixion and death of Christ on this reverent day. Last year, I watched the movie "The Passion of the Christ" in anticipation and celebration of Easter. If you have not seen the movie, the vivid scenes are heartbreaking watching the pain that was inflicted on Christ as He stood as an innocent substitute for the guilty. He was bruised, beaten and battered and His flesh was ripped off exposing His internal organs. Something is happening in me that is difficult to express. It is painful and lovely all at the same time. I feel layer after layer being ripped off my heart and soul exposing things in my life, my character that I sometimes am too afraid or too ashamed to look at. I know that this exposure is necessary. It has been an ongoing process for me for years really, but I know I must peel away everything that hides my loving heart.

When I was a little girl, we had a boy in our group named Chuck that was a friend of my brother's. Chuck's greatest desire was to be muscular and buff. Even as a young boy, he worked out with his uncle and lifted weights constantly. Having bulging muscles just did something to make him feel good about himself. I could relate to Chuck. Sitting at my piano, with lovely melodies shooting from my fingers like rays of sunshine, made me feel good about myself also. Sometimes, Chuck thought that his muscles still weren't big enough, so he would pile on layer after layer of clothes to puff up just a bit more. Poor little fella... he might have on four or five shirts or sweaters, even in warm weather just so he could look muscle-bound! Last year, some of my childhood friends and I got together with a "reunion" of sorts from our "gang" from childhood. We all talked about Chuck. It was a bittersweet moment for all of us, as our friend had passed away just a few years ago in his forties. After he grew up, he was somewhat overweight and ended up with a bad heart. How sad that the very body he proudly displayed as a child ended up being his worst enemy.

I suppose I had been no different than Chuck. When I was a girl, I sometimes did not like what I saw in the mirror. It had been a struggle ever since that first day I came home with my eyeglasses. Of course what I did not know back then was every girl felt the way I did, every girl had a battle with what they saw in the mirror at times - even the most popular ones. We all battle insecurities of one sort or another. The truth be known, it is much more about what is behind the face in the mirror that is actually reflected there. My insecurities stemmed from an insatiable need for acceptance. I wanted to "fit in," to feel "normal." I had watched other girls getting the boyfriends and going on dates. It seemed effortless. Well, I did excel in one category. I was one amazing friend for both boys and girls - the one that they ran to with problems, the one they used as a shoulder to cry on when they needed it. Goodness, what a compliment and honor that was and I didn't even realize it! Now I understand and wouldn't trade a listening ear and compassionate heart for all the beauty in Hollywood, but back then I would've traded a pretty face for some of those things that were not as easily seen. Funny how an insecure heart can distort one's thinking. I tried very hard not to allow my friends and classmates see that conflicted little girl inside. I was so afraid of what they would see. So, I hid behind a caring smile and a listening ear.

When I left for college, I experienced changes - drastic changes as we often do on our journey towards adulthood. I acquired a prescription for contact lenses and stashed away those hideous glasses that always made me feel less than beautiful. I cut my hair and began wearing more stylish clothes. To my surprise, I did have a cute figure after all. I felt that no one had seemed to notice before. I confess… I liked the attention. Soon, that attention began to define me more and more and wrap layer after layer around that beautiful heart deep inside of me. If I had a "bad hair day," it affected my perception. If I had a "good hair day" and no one noticed, I put extra effort into my looks to make sure they would. Oh the money I could've saved in hairspray alone! Before long, I equated "love" with attraction. What a web I had wound around myself. My beautiful heart was covered by lipstick and hairspray, it seemed. When low self-esteem that had haunted me since childhood reared its ugly head, I worried more and more about what others saw with their eyes rather than felt with their heart. Then the inevitable happened - I settled for much less than I deserved or desired. That choice led to a relationship laced with abuse and abandonment that only served to wrap me in an even deeper web, building layer after layer, both to hide and to protect my hurting heart. What followed that first marriage was a series of broken relationships and hurt - more hurt than I ever dreamed possible.

Sometimes when we are hurt by those who are supposed to love us most, it leaves scars that we simply feel we must cover and hide and protect. We feel ugly and ashamed, and long even more for someone to think we are beautiful "scars and all." As a broken young woman dealing with an abusive marriage, I had wrapped many layers around my heart. I couldn't bear to look at the scars myself, let alone find courage enough to let others see them. One night in particular, still haunts me with so many questions as to how another person could be so cruel and think so little of the person they profess love for. Even though the abuse only came during moments of inebriation, I still could not understand how my husband could be so removed from the hurt and pain he caused me. Substance abuse takes one further than they ever intended to go. Because of this cruel abuse at my husband's hands, I delivered our baby three months premature. My son was only a few weeks old fighting for his life in the neonatal unit of the hospital. Every time I looked at his tiny little body, my heart would break and I was determined to be there for him, no matter what. The truth is, without this miracle, this gift in my life, I saw little reason to live or to keep trying. The doctor's had told me that I was to rest, not climb stairs and to take time to properly heal from the delivery. The stitches I had were a reminder to me of how fragile my little one was. My husband and I lived on the second floor of an apartment building, so avoiding stairs was impossible for me if I were going to visit my precious baby boy in the hospital each day. Also, I was delivering breast milk daily to try and boost his immune system and strengthen his digestive tract to where he could eat rather than being constantly fed through an IV. My health was the last thing I was concerned about. It had only been a few weeks since the delivery and procedure, but my husband thought it had been way too long - too long for what his inebriated mind needed. He was back on his drinking and drugging binges before I had even left the hospital. He escaped his fear over our baby's fate in his old familiar way. One evening, he staggered in to our apartment during the wee hours of the night. He wanted his wife and wanted me then. I explained to him that we must wait because I had not healed and it was not safe. He was like a ravenous animal, not caring for anything more than his basic carnal needs. I begged, I pleaded but to no avail. I closed my mind off to what was happening and prayed for help, for deliverance. Then ... it was over. I wanted to run, I wanted to scream, I wanted to have him arrested and I wanted to tell someone - ANYONE. What good would it do? Who would believe me? No one really knew the depth of his rage. He had become master at hiding his sins. This was just another one of those nights. I was his to have anytime he wanted and needed. *Instead of trying to escape his abuse, I cried silently into the night until exhaustion gave way to sleep.*

Yes, I feel exposed today. That trauma was so many years go, yet scars that I thought no longer existed still remain. The truth is, I have covered them with emotional "shirts and sweaters" like our friend Chuck - *trying desperately to look beautiful, to feel beautiful and to be okay.* I thought I had exposed them all, but once again more scars are revealed by the light of love deep in my heart. It seems that just with physical healing, emotional healing is a process. It takes time and that is okay. I must trust the process and allow my heart room to heal and grow strong again. I can't deny the truth. Sometimes, I still feed that deep need to feel beautiful on the outside as a way to distract some of the things still healing on the inside. It seems that need for validation gnaws at the deepest part of my being, at times. I suppose we all experience this need now and again. Yet even through moments of attention, attraction and affirmation, the raw truth remains. Being desired on a superficial level cannot fill the longings deep within our hearts. No matter how much I have desired to cover them, I do have scars - they aren't pretty, but what I am beginning to understand is that they are what actually make me beautiful in the ways that truly matter. I do not need to allow physical attraction feed my fear of being unloved. Attraction is a deceptive tool in the hands of hurting hearts. Attraction cannot make another person love me. I have fallen prey to its deception too many times. Some people use attraction to solicit love and others use it to avoid love, but it is still the same - "shirts and sweaters" masking fearful, lonely, hurting hearts. Sometime ago, a friend and I were talking about our thoughts on inner and outer beauty. Part of me grieves because I sometimes ignore the very lesson I try to teach others, and because I have not fully allowed others to see what I long for them to see. In our conversation, my friend told me that he does see in me what I long for everyone to see, but it is I who sometimes struggles with seeing what others see in me. This beauty that he compliments me on so often is only "wrapping" for the true gift inside - a beautiful heart mended by grace and filled with love... Many layers have been peeled off today.

CHAPTER 9

COVER GIRL

"It was on an early morning like today that I put my 'cover girl' face to the ultimate test. The night had been literal hell. One moment I thought I was going to die and another moment wished that I would. Abuse and addiction had reared their ugly head and I had been the brunt of it all again."

It is early morning and the house is strangely quiet. I take a moment to breathe in the stillness, it is so rare. The sun has not shown its face yet. Across the room I see a reflection of myself staring back at me from my dresser mirror. That is a woman no one ever sees - no make up, hair in a ponytail, glasses parked on the edge of my nose - certainly not the face of "Cover Girl." For as long as I can remember, I have been a "cover girl" in one way or another. It wasn't until recently that I found the courage to go an entire day without make-up when others were around to see. I have always been of the opinion that even old barns look better with a coat of paint. Now mind you, I still cannot leave the house without my "face" on. I think it is my southern upbringing. A southern belle would never be caught dead walking through the door of her beauty salon without washed and styled hair and heaven forbid that she show up for a manicure without a fresh coat of polish on perfectly filed nails! To this day, my mom does not even come to the breakfast table until she has brushed up her hair, brushed her teeth and is fully dressed. "June Cleaver" simply would not lounge around in her PJ's all morning - heaven's no! As for me though, I am slowly finding a strange comfort in my natural beauty while hanging out at home. I think it has something to do with hitting middle age. It takes awhile to feel at home in one's own skin. Perhaps it is like wearing leather shoes. They are a bit stiff when you first put them on, but through the wear and tear of "time" they soften up and become comfortable! I am like that "old pair of shoes" - finding bliss and beauty that has escaped me for years. Now, I am beginning to feel beautiful even on days like this - bare freckled face and all. I have to admit, I've seen a glow that has been hidden for more years than I can count. It is quite calming to be comfortable in my own skin for a change. For too long, I've been like a visitor in my own body.

From the time I was a young girl, we were assigned weekly chores. I fully believe that every child needs to be given degrees of responsibility early on. Each week, I would make the beds, help out in the kitchen cooking and washing dishes, and would finally tackle the most daunting of all - dusting the furniture. This was before the days of those "Swiffer wands" where you just swipe around everything. No, I had to take every item off the furniture, spray it down with polish, and wipe with a cloth to a shine. That scent of lemon "Pledge" still nauseates my senses to this day! Covering the entire house took hours, but this was my Saturday morning task. There was no TV, playing in the yard or house, talking on the phone or listening to the radio until I had successfully completed all of my chores. My brother found ways around his often, but not me. Perhaps that was his advantage of being the baby of the family. Aside from these privileges, most of all, there was the "allowance" that I earned. I knew exactly where my money would be spent. For years, my money was invested into the corner store in candy "stock" - jolly ranchers, dreamcicles, now-and-laters, cream sodas, bottle caps, orange crushes, pixie sticks... As puberty kicked in, I realized that my allowance was my ticket out of being that awkward, freckle faced girl that stared at me each day. I slipped out and purchased my first cosmetics. How pretty that girl in the mirror was even behind those ugly glasses! I remembered her from days gone by. Since I was just a novice at the art of applying make-up, it didn't take long for my parents to see what I had done with my money. Oh what a battle of the wills that transpired - the first of many, but for then, the "Cover Girl" was there to stay.

"Cover Girl" - I think I've often been a "cover girl" even without make-up... masking fears, hurts and insecurities. I had become so proficient at hiding behind my "million dollar smile" that no one ever saw all the scars carved deep in my heart. It is amazing what a forced smile can cover. *It was on an early morning like today that I put my "cover girl" face to the ultimate test. The night had been literal hell. One moment I thought I was going to die and another moment wished that I would. Abuse and addiction had reared their ugly head and I had been the brunt of it all again.* At some point, all of the slaps to my face became a blur as my head beat against the wall behind my bed with each blow. *"Oh God"* I cried out. Over and over I cried and pleaded as the burning pain to my face and head mingled with the stinging tears flowing down my bruised cheeks. I looked up into the face of the "stranger" who had me pinned to the bed. The voice of a "demon" replied with a laugh through my husband's lips. *"Ha! Where's your God now?"* Sometime in the wee hours of the morning, I gave in to sleep from sheer exhaustion. I had only been asleep for a short while when the phone rang. Mom had been in a terrible accident on her way to work. Slowly, I slipped out of bed so as not to wake my spouse, the addict. Life was bearable when he slept. My feet hit the floor like concrete blocks and my head felt like a lead balloon. Hesitantly, I peered into the mirror on the wall. *"Oh dear God!"* I had no idea who this battered woman was staring back at me with this black and blue bruised swollen face. What would I do now? I had to get to the hospital but I couldn't go like this. I looked like the one who had been in an accident. More like a train wreck - a train wreck of a life so it seemed. If I had ever needed a miracle, today was it. I reached for my make-up bag. I could only hope that "Cover Girl" would live up to its name.

Amazingly, no one knew that day. Amazingly, no one knew many days. Even on days when the pain was only internal, no one knew. What a daunting task it was to apply that mask each day. I wore it for so long that I could not even see myself when I looked into a mirror or into my own heart. For years I hid behind a thick "Cover Girl" layer. Suitors didn't see beyond it, companions couldn't get past it and I was too afraid to wash it away. As I write today, however, I look up at that face in the mirror staring at me. Today, she smiles back - not a "cover girl" smile, but a smile that radiates from within. Suddenly, I feel very inspired and ready to make it a full day of it in my "natural state." A perfect "writer's day" is unfolding. For you "non writers," that is a day when beauty goes out the window, housework is put on the back burner, and eating healthy seems a bit lower on the noble list of priorities. The passion in you drives you with a focus that is all but impossible to break. You are like a laser - or like a race horse with blinders on - nothing else matters other than letting those ideas give birth to words on a page that are meant to take wings and fly.

I wish I could tell you that all those "Cover Girl" days were due to my southern belle way of thinking, but that was only a part of it. The other? It was fear - plain and simple. My self-esteem had been whittled down to the point to where I could not even look at myself. I imagine we all have had times in life just like this. We long to look beautiful, feel beautiful and be beautiful. I wasn't just covering "freckles and blemishes" with my "Cover Girl," but sometimes covering thoughts and attitudes. So many non-productive hours were spent focusing on externals to hide the internals. At some point though, I realized that I could not allow "Cover Girl" to forever mask what was deep within. As a writer, I find it imperative to be transparent with my thoughts so that my words ring of authenticity. I confess, at times it has been a greater challenge than at others. Writers aren't any different than anyone else. Sometimes, we are afraid to face some of our own emotions or thoughts, so we fight not to gauge our words when sharing some of the deepest expressions of the heart. The thing is, if we can't express those things, then the readers certainly won't gain much from what we write other than superficial entertainment. But I stray from my point. The point is, each of us has a need to feel beautiful/handsome, to be perceived as beautiful/handsome inside and out, and sometimes we become "cover girls" or "macho men" to help form that perception in the minds of others. So, on days such as my writer's day, or a day when we are sad or angry or hurt or irritable we feel less than beautiful/handsome. That begs the question, is it truly because of others' perception or our own?

I have a two fold answer to that in the form of two stories. A couple of months ago my cousin Tiffany posted a picture of herself after a long day of working in the yard with her sweet husband Trent. She was six months pregnant and covered in layers of dirt! She felt confident to show everyone her less than perfect self. Why? Because she is happy with her life, with whom she is and even more she has a man that adores her and loves her even on "digging in the dirt" days. Tiffany and I have had some similar life experiences so I totally understand her lovely, peaceful, happy and beautiful heart and outlook. She is adorable!

Secondly, I recall a time in my own life. As I have already shared, several years ago I faced a difficult time of illness. Besides the chronic migraine and the neuropathy that was caused along the right side of my body, my right eye began to cross and over a period of a couple of years, was severely crossed. It was devastating for me because I had truly worked long and hard to overcome those negative feelings about myself and to feel beautiful inside and out again. Just about the time I did, this condition manifested itself and the struggle with self-esteem began all over again. That one physical flaw caused me to face internal demons one more time. The irony of it all was that those close to me, and even people I didn't really know, seemed to think I was beautiful. I didn't have problems dating or relating to people in business or even social environments, but every once in awhile, I would look in the mirror and be less than happy with the woman I saw. Memories of abuse, abandonment and belittlement haunted me once more. When I had pictures taken of myself, I would cover that crossed right eye with my long hair. It made me feel safe and happy. I was covering a "flaw" that cut at me like a knife. When I was in a store or in public somewhere, I never could look people in the eye. Last November, I had the opportunity to get surgery on that eye that not only corrected the issue, but actually improved my vision greatly. I had lost much of that vision with my childhood injury. The day of the surgery, a close male friend of mine asked if he could be the one to take me to the hospital. I wanted him there. I needed him close. Over the years, he had told me how beautiful I was, how amazing I was. Still, on the day of the surgery I felt so insecure, so vulnerable. I wasn't allowed to wear any makeup that day and he would see me "au naturel!" When he picked me up, I let him in but would not even look him in the eye. As soon as we got to the front door, I put on sunglasses. Even as we sat in the hospital waiting, I kept the glasses on part time. When I was taken back and put in a hospital bed, he came back and kissed me on the cheek and told me everything would be okay.

If I thought I had looked less than perfect before the surgery, after the surgery trumped that by a long shot. I had this blood red eye that looked like Frankenstein's sister! Days and weeks passed, however, and my eye healed. It was straight! As I began to truly look at myself in the mirror, I also began to "see" myself. Things that I thought were long gone, surfaced.

I faced internal things that had been tucked so far down in my heart and soul that it took an emotional crow bar to pry them loose. Little by little, day by day, I began to give myself genuine love and acceptance. One day I was talking to my friend. He was complimenting me on my beauty again like he had so many times before. (Every woman needs a male friend like this!) He had seen a picture of me in my Sunday finest. He said *"you have that beautiful thing going on."* Then he clarified and said *"I've seen you all dressed up on Sunday, fixed up for a date, hanging out at home, hair all tousled and a mess or slicked back in a ponytail, makeup worn off at the end of a day and even no makeup the day of your surgery and in every case you had that beautiful thing going on."* He was right. He had seen me in all those states, but had also seen me in all of my emotional states as well - happy, sad, fearful, peaceful, loving, callous, angry, joyful, laughing, crying... As we were talking, I was actually standing in the bathroom and looking at myself in the mirror. You know, for the first time, truly and completely, I agreed with him. Not because of what I saw, but what I felt and knew. I had found the capacity to both love and be loved - to give acceptance knowing that I was accepted. I realized more than ever that beauty was more than a painted on smile; it was a glow from deep in my heart. Yes he was right; I did have "that beautiful thing" going on! Looking in the mirror that day I felt the same feeling I did this morning seeing myself in the mirror. There is no longer a stranger staring back at me behind a "Cover Girl" mask. I know that beautiful, brown-eyed, freckled face girl...

CHAPTER 10

LOOK WHAT I DID!

"I felt that little hand tugging on my bed covers and that sweet voice whispering in my ear. 'Get up Mommy. Please get up. Come here I want to show you something!' Obediently, I got up from bed and followed my little one into his room. 'Look what I did Mommy! I know it's kinda crooked but I tried. I wanted to show you what I did. I did it for you!'..."

For the last few years a regular topic around our family table has been sports. My nephew Byron played high school football and headed off for college to play ball and has this common bond with my dad since he, too, played football in high school. Most recently, my seventy-four year old mother began reading the Sports page. I am still in shock over that one. There are frequent discussions about who did what, who lost, who won, who received an offer, etc. Everyone in their own way seeks affirmation in those areas that are important to them. It might be something such as *"Did you see how good the yard looked?"* or *"How did you enjoy the meal I cooked?"* Sometimes Joshua will wash my car, stroll in with a big grin on his face and ask *"how does it look?"* My grown boy still needs affirmation. We all have that inner child that longs for appreciation and wants to be noticed. What we often forget is that this isn't about perfection; it is about effort and appreciation. It is about motives of the heart. Understanding this need for affirmation and what drives it has been a lesson in progress for me on my quest for healthy self-esteem. It is a lesson that is slowly teaching me how to peel off the layers of my heart and take off the mask of my soul. I am beginning to understand that others can not possibly see the longings of my heart if I keep them buried so deeply.

Sometimes, when I watch my son as he helps me around my house and then flashes that big grin that makes my heart melt, I see myself in his eyes. Yes, he is so much a reflection of me and always has been from the time he was a little boy - the little giver, the doer, the encourager. Perhaps he learned a little too well how to wear a painted on smile, a mask that often hid that need for approval, for affirmation. This is not exactly something I wanted him to learn, but yet I am so overjoyed at his giving nature and caring disposition. When he was about five years old, Joshua did what most children do at his age. He woke up early on a Saturday morning. You can't pry them out of bed on a school day, but on the weekends their little feet hit the floor as soon as the sun is up - the few days when parents can sleep late. This particular Saturday, I was attempting a "sleep in" knowing it would most likely be a futile effort. Not to my surprise, *I felt that little hand tugging on my bed covers and that sweet voice whispering in my ear. "Get up Mommy. Please get up. Come here I want to show you something!" Obediently, I got up from bed and followed my little one into his room. "Look what I did Mommy! I know it's kinda crooked but I tried. I wanted to show you what I did. I did it for you!"* What my son had shown me was his heartfelt attempt at making his own bed for the very first time. Now, mind you, I am a bit of a perfectionist. When I make a bed, all the wrinkles have to be smoothed out, the comforter must be hanging even on both sides and the pillows must be ever so carefully placed in a symmetrical order. My precious little boy's bed was anything but what I just described. The comforter was crooked and uneven, the pillows were tossed sporadically on the bed and the sheet hung longer than the comforter in spots. But to me that day, it was perfect! Why? Because my little Josh did his very best. He attempted something that he knew would please me and this was his only motive. *"Oh Joshua it is wonderful!"* I hugged that little brown-eyed angel and had to walk into my room to wipe away a tear. I thought about my own life and how many times things I had done turned out crooked and wrinkled. Even when I was giving it my all! Sometimes I did get that proverbial "hug" and other times not. It is the "nots" that knock us for a loop and cause the legs of our self esteem to be a bit shaky and sends our whittled down egos running in circles in an attempt to please others. I had become such a perfectionist.

When I was a little girl and taking piano lessons, practicing was never a real issue for me. I loved the piano! I loved the way I felt when I was achieving something others around me could not or would not. It was my secret little world, my magic kingdom where I was princess. My parents were very busy people - with their jobs, with family, with volunteering in their local church… taking care of everyone and everything it seemed to me. In their "busyness," it meant even more to me when Mom or Dad would take time to peek their head in the living room while I was strolling up and down the piano keys. Mom would sit and listen or Dad would flash that handsome smile. Then the icing on the cake was when I would go for my weekly piano lesson. If I had mastered one of my musical pieces, my teacher would put a gold star at the top of the page in my music book. A star! I pretended I was a star - a famous star. My piano teacher was a very wise woman. If the truth be told, she would give gold stars even before I had totally mastered some of the more difficult songs. She knew the importance of affirmation. Encouragement goes a long way. Perhaps my teacher understood how much that shy little girl with the amazing dexterity in her hands needed someone to acknowledge her hard work and accomplishments. Can I confess? When that little girl grew up, she never stopped longing for someone to notice. I had spent my whole life "performing" in one way or another so that someone would take note. None of us ever really do stop longing for that affirmation, do we? I wondered if anyone had ever truly seen what was behind that smile as bright as a star and what was deep inside that heart pure as snow. Thinking back on how hard I tried to please others and still try at times, I see even more how much my grown son acted out the same performance as a child and continues to do so as an adult. He wears a smile that totally melts my heart, extends a hand of love and care to everyone around him despite his own need for a hand to hold tight to. I had tried to be both Mom and Dad to him as he was growing up, but there was only so much I could do. The absence of a father had put quite a heavy load on his small shoulders way back when. Parents can never underestimate the impact their time and attention or lack thereof makes on their children. Just watch what a child does and how he acts both negatively or positively and you can truly see what type of impact you've made on your child. That impact carries over into adulthood without a doubt. I know it did for me. Yes, Josh was so much like me. I had always had that heart to please others and make them proud and he was like a "mini me."

One Sunday, I was scheduled to sing a solo in the morning worship service. I had already taught a Sunday school class, sang on the worship team, was sitting in the choir participating in the music program and was next up to sing after the offertory. Frankly, I was exhausted. I truly had been performing all my life. I came from a long line of "doers." That morning, I had on a new dress and thought I looked rather nice. Right before I was set to sing, my mother the retired choir director leaned over to me and said *"That's a nice dress. It's pretty but you might want to hold your shoulders up a bit when you get up on stage; your stomach is a little puffy this morning."* I knew she meant well, that's what moms do, (and I've done the same thing I suppose with my son over things), but any thoughts of worship in the song went out the window and all I could think of was my "puffy" stomach. I was only about 110 pounds soaking wet, but I had a puffy stomach! Never mind that I had eloquently delivered a Sunday school lesson, had participated as a part of the worship team and was using my talent in the choir as well. Never mind that I felt pretty with a new dress because I so rarely got them on my budget. We all use what we have been gifted with, hoping that someone will notice, someone will benefit from what we contribute. Ninety-nine good deeds can be done and one bad, and people only remember the one. It's just human nature. Ever heard of Achilles? In Greek mythology he was an incredible warrior that was undefeated, but the only thing people remember about this character is his weak "heel." Because his heel was unprotected, he was hit by an arrow, knocked to his knees and defeated.

Sometimes it takes many years to realize that we are not the sum total of all the things we do. What we do is just that - what we do. It is not who we are deep inside. Perhaps as I write this story and others the "inner child" in me cries out - *"look what I did... aren't you proud of me?"* Something stirs in my heart even as I type those words. I hear a familiar voice whispering in my soul - *"Oh Starla it is wonderful!"* I feel STRONG arms holding me close. I am loved, crooked comforter and all.

CHAPTER 11

UPHILL CLIMB

"I felt so alone, that is, until I reached for my belly where I felt the miracle that was growing inside. Had it not been for my sweet baby, I would've gladly given up the ghost. My little 'fighter' hung on for three more months before he made his grand entrance. He came in only twenty-six weeks of my pregnancy. The first three months were truly a fight for life for my little one..."

Let me reiterate a few simple facts about myself. I am not an athlete, I am a girly girl. I am stubborn and often refuse to give in, but at the same time, I will give all in anything I am asked to do. I have fallen, but have not failed, because I get up and refuse to give up. The girl who used to be shy, now talks too much and listens too little. I am outspoken, but have a difficult time speaking up for myself. I have a heart the size of Texas, crowding a five feet one and half inch frame. I am tough as nails, but vulnerable as a lamb. I trust too much, but then don't trust at all. I have small shoulders, but sometimes carry the weight of the world. I don't always "get it right" but it isn't for lack of effort. I just felt the need for an exercise in transparency today! It is ever an uphill climb isn't it?

During that "life altering" decision so many years ago, I tried everything to make a doomed marriage work. One venture involved trying to go into business with my spouse just to stay as close as I could to him to keep him distracted from his addictive lifestyle. We were running, what was affectionately called by the industrial complexes, a "roach coach." We catered breakfast and lunch in a little truck to various companies and industrial sites. Our truck was not a new one and rolled out oftentimes on a wing and a prayer. Each morning, I would get up around three a.m. to make biscuits, sausage, bacon, toast and eggs to compile the breakfast sandwiches we sold. I would shrink wrap them, price them and load them on trays for the truck. I would make sure all the cold sandwiches, salads and gallons of tea that I had prepared the night before were ready to go. Often, I would also make chili, soup and various other hot meals - all of this before six a.m. when it was time to load the truck for the day. One morning, everything was ready and loaded. I said a quick *"goodbye"* to my husband and was getting ready to go back to bed for an hour before I had to start all over again. On this particular morning, the old truck just wanted to "go back to bed" too. It simply would not start. It was a heavy one ton truck and our driveway was a steep hill. As I watched out the window, I saw my spouse as he took my car and parked it in front of the truck. He tied a rope from the back of the car to the truck so he could pull it uphill to jump start the "roach coach." What he did not realize was how heavy the truck was in comparison to the car. In a moment, the rope snapped. He panicked as he saw the truck rolling downhill towards the garage. Without thinking, he jumped out of the car to chase the truck, leaving the car in drive. I heard a loud "thud" as the house rattled from the truck's impact and watched as my car strolled across the street and landed in my neighbor's front yard like a wounded animal. All of this, while my husband stood between the two of them with his hands in the air. That day the scene was like watching a Saturday Night Live sketch. I actually laughed until I cried as I watched this hilarious event unfold. Truly though, there was nothing humorous in his behavior. It was tragic. I had offered to help but he refused; certainly not the first time, but one of many that sadly led to a last time once and for all for him.

It still seems surreal that the day finally came years later when my husband took his last breath because of his addiction. Forty-three years old, he spent his last hours alienated from those who loved him still refusing help from God or man. We had been divorced for about three years when I received the news. He had been picked up for "public drunk" on a street corner, put in a jail cell to dry out overnight. The next morning when the guards came to check on him, he was dead. The autopsy stated that he died of a "severe fatty liver." He had abandoned everyone and everything to chase after the one thing he least needed; the one thing that finally took everything from him, even his life eventually. I had warned him years before. I actually had a dream where I literally saw his outcome. He laughed it off and said he would live forever. I carried guilt for years being torn between grief and relief. His personal torment weighed heavy on his mind and spirit, and as a result, tormented everyone who loved him. It was almost a relief that he was no longer having to fight his internal demons. His spirit had been so willing, but his flesh had been way too weak. My prayer was that somehow through it all, he finally was at peace. He had helped hundreds of others turn their lives around and conquer their addictions, yet he had never been able to help himself.

I had not made the decision lightly to leave him those years before. When he was sober, he was the most loving, attentive husband a girl could ask for. We were a great team in service to others and in life. When addiction reared its nasty head, however, my husband's alter ego took over much like Dr. Jekyll and Mr. Hyde. As long as it was just the two of us, I stayed through thick and thin, enduring unspeakable hurt and pain, being belittled and left alone to suffer in silence time and time again. Something changed, though, once my sweet little preemie baby boy arrived. It took some time, but I began walking that road towards freedom from fear and hurt in my mind and heart. The change began to take place months before my sweet boy was even born. I had only been pregnant for three months when another binge week came along that resulted in a visit to the hospital for myself. I still remember the night like it was yesterday and it was over twenty-one years ago. My husband was late coming home from work and I knew what that meant. He would not be in good form when he did return home. I had learned how to appease him. If I stayed very quiet, didn't ask questions and was non-confrontational, I usually survived the night unscathed. That night however, he seemed ready for a fight. He was antagonistic and confrontational. He pushed my buttons in every way imaginable. When I would not argue back with him, he began picking things up and breaking them. He even took a painting off the wall and smashed it. He knew how much our lovely little serene apartment meant to me. It was a refuge in the middle of the wilderness. Unsettling this refuge was how he could hurt me and "ruffle my feathers." For many years, I relived the anguish again and again… the screaming, the violent display, the sound of broken glass, furniture being knocked over and then the surreal moment as I felt myself tumbling through the air over the sofa. It is quite odd how our minds can go into such a quiet protective mode as such drama ensues. I sat strangely calm as I watched my husband walk out the door; not only did I not feel any pain, I did not feel anything. I was completely numb. Robotically, I picked up the phone and called friends of ours for help. After a visit to the hospital, I returned home, crawled into bed and drifted off to sleep from sheer exhaustion. *I felt so alone, that is, until I reached for my belly where I felt the miracle that was growing inside. Had it not been for my sweet baby, I would've gladly given up the ghost. My little "fighter" hung on for three more months before he made his grand entrance. He came in only twenty-six weeks of my pregnancy. The first three months were truly a fight for life for my little one,* but that gentle voice deep within reminded me that we were not alone on this journey and I never stopped believing that my little angel would make it through. Nothing much changed with my husband. He was back out on the streets nursing his own hurt and pain before I even left the hospital. It wasn't that he didn't love me or our son; he just could not love himself enough to find the courage to face the truth deep in his heart. After three long months of daily visits to the hospital, I was able to finally walk out its front doors with my gift from above.

Time rocked on and Joshua grew. He was such a tiny thing for a very long time. There were lovely days and not so lovely days, but in it all, I never gave up. Each morning that I woke and looked into that sweet little face, I had a reason to keep going, keep fighting and keep believing. There were actually days that we had behaved like a real family - mommy, daddy and baby; then came the binges. My husband was forever trying to pull the weight of our lives uphill in his own feeble strength and it simply was not enough. One evening he was late coming home from work - again. I went about my nightly routine. I sat with Josh in my arms and rocked him gently, singing his favorite lullaby. *"You are my sunshine, my only sunshine..."* Holding him close, smelling that fresh baby scent, touching his soft skin and stroking the silky locks of his dark brown hair had a way of melting away all the pain and sadness from my life with his father. I cradled him in my arms and gently laid him in his crib so as not to wake him. Dutifully, I went back to the living room and waited for my husband to come home. Part of me prayed he would so I would know he was safe and the other part of me hoped he never returned. None too soon, I heard the familiar turn of the key in the lock. He staggered in with that glassy expression on his face and spoke briefly through slurred lips. Thankfully, he was not in the mood for confrontation, so he quietly slipped into the bedroom and passed out on the bed. Wearily, I took a deep breath and carefully shut our bedroom door. I stepped into the nursery to check on the baby. As I reached down to stroke his little forehead, I accidentally bumped the musical mobile hanging over the crib. The tiny jingle disrupted my little one's peaceful dreams and he began to cry. I quickly scooped him up in my arms trying desperately to soothe his cries before the inevitable happened. It was too late, however. The door to the nursery flung open and my husband pounced into the room like a hungry lion ready for the kill. He snatched our little boy out of my arms and began slapping him on his little legs. *"Shut up! Shut up! Shut up!"* Josh, screamed all the louder. At that moment every fear that I had held deep within dissipated and tenacity rose up in me. My own animal instincts kicked in - that of a mama bear protecting her cub. *"GIVE ME MY BABY and don't you DARE touch him or me EVER again!"* I was ready to die, but at least die fighting. To my surprise, my husband pulled away, methodically turned and walked back to the bedroom and passed out again on the bed totally oblivious to his own actions. He loved that little boy, so I was certain if he had been the least bit aware of his behavior towards our sweet baby, he would've felt immeasurable guilt and hurt. He had been without his father throughout life and wanted so desperately to be a real father to our son. I wrapped my arms tightly around my precious little one, walked into the living room and carefully laid down on the sofa, laying Joshua on my chest and gingerly stroking his back. His little legs were a beet red - almost the color of anger that was painted across my face. He was so traumatized that his cry was nothing more than a soft whimper. We both cried into the night until exhaustion gave way to sleep. I had kept so much from my family, but the next day as soon as my husband left the house, I packed my bags, called my parents and walked out of the "hell" that we had endured once and for all.

To this day, fears from those years still haunt me in my dreams on rare occasions. I am reminded that the affects from abuse never really die even if the abuser does. I recently connected with a woman who was abused in her teens and early adulthood. She is in her fifties now and has a wonderful life with a beautiful family, but she still carries that fear in the back of her mind and deep in her heart. I've met many women and a few men over the years who carry that same burden of fear. I am just so grateful that even the most difficult of life experiences can be used for good as a reminder for others. We are not alone on this journey! I believe we are designed to help each other along the path, up the hill, through the valley - wherever we find ourselves in life. Thinking back to those years before of the day I watched my husband try to get that truck up the little hill in our driveway, I wonder about some of my own actions that seemed so futile. How many times had I been like that little car the day my husband tried to jump off the truck - trying to pull a heavy load much larger than I uphill? Life is sometimes an uphill climb. Mine certainly had been one long continuous climb. Admit it or not, we either have to lighten the load or accept help. My day of epiphany, the day I walked out of my house and left my husband was one of those days for me.

About six years ago, I began a routine of walking. My idea of exercise had been walking in the mall! I began walking with a friend of mine who was considered a "jock." He and I walked together at least once a week. I eventually built up a great deal of endurance over time. One of my favorite places to go walking was on the beach. On one particular day, we had been walking for hours. We walked the beach and even climbed the hills and walked in and out of the old fort there. On our return towards the beach, we decided to take the "high road" - literally. There was a steep hill that was almost straight up from the highway that led back to the beach. I had not missed a beat through our long trek through the sand and even our exploration of the old fort. I was exhausted, but this stubborn "girly girl" was not about to show weakness! Halfway up that hill however, I felt as if I was carrying a halfback on my shoulders and thought my heart was going to explode. Finally, I sheepishly asked for some relief and help. Asking for help is something that I have never been gifted at. We stopped to rest and then he helped me the remaining way up that hill. That hill is so reflective of my life. Perhaps it is because most of my adult life I've felt as if I was carrying all the load uphill by myself while those who committed to sharing the load were really just along for the ride. I suppose I have just wanted someone for once to say *"I know you're tired, let me carry it for awhile."* At times, I have looked at my "invisible hill" and wished that someone would not just "help" me up the hill or carry my load for awhile, but carry ME. Sometimes, I've been tired and wanted to crawl up in someone's lap to be held, loved and protected; I've just longed for someone to allow me the freedom to rest, if just but for a moment. Even with that desire and even on days when loved ones have supported me and held me up, I've come to realize and understand that it is not their job; it is not their "hill." It is MY hill and I must climb it.

That hill by the beach rather adequately describes life - one uphill climb after another. We are on a journey to a higher place than where we were yesterday. Like my little car in our driveway all those years ago, I have had to break away from loads that are too heavy for me. At times, I have felt the invisible hands of my Maker pull me up when I had no strength left on my own. Again, I am reminded that success is not about a destination, but a journey. As that song says *"it's the climb."* Perhaps each time that I stretch my legs up that hill, I am growing stronger than I realize.

ROLLER COASTER

"We helped her to her feet. Her silver hair was tossed towards her face, and her glasses lay crooked on her nose like a wrecked bicycle. It took a while, but eventually that sweet, silly smile of hers cracked open her lips and then came that wide-open hearty laugh. I didn't want to admit it, but although I enjoyed the ride, I was also glad when it came to a stop."

Emotions… they without a doubt have to be the most fickle thing known to humans. In the course of the day, I have run the gamut of emotions like the ivories on my piano. Perhaps it's life and perhaps it's only hormones! Who knows? At the end of a day it is easy to feel like I've just stepped off of a roller coaster. Or yet still on one, yelling *"Stop! I want to get off!"* Actually, I began to write about this very thing a few years ago. We've all just wanted to "jump ship" on more than one occasion. Life's ups and downs, spins and flips are like a roller coaster ride at times. The ride of life is often fast pace with unexpected twists and turns. It is easy to get knocked for a loop. At times, we all feel as if we are stopping to allow our hearts to catch up with our bodies before the next turn. There is something to that saying *"I felt my heart jump up in my throat."* Life truly is a thrill and a challenge. Sometimes, we climb an exciting hill of college, of marriage, having children or embarking on a career, and then find ourselves at other times speeding down a hill of divorce or around a curve of sickness or through a dark tunnel of losing a job. Up and down, high and low, in and out we go like a roller coaster on vacation at a theme park somewhere. It is exciting fearful, exhilarating, exhausting all in the space of a few moments, it seems. It is a ride that will take us to our destination if we will try to relax and get the most out it.

Growing up, the word "vacation" for us was synonymous with "Mama Rich and Paw Paw." Anytime my parents had vacation from work or had a holiday, we would hop in the car and travel to my grandparents in North Alabama. Mama Rich was one of those hard working women who still always found time to laugh and enjoy life. She was a jolly woman, this woman whose hands I see as I look at mine. She had shiny silver hair and an infectious smile. What we would consider routine, she viewed as special. Every visit to my grandparents always involved a special day trip to "town." The women and children would pile in the car and head towards town for a morning of shopping at Grant's Department Store and then lunch at Captain D's. Mama Rich loved Captain D's. Most anything was tasty to her simply because she did not have to cook! Aside from these spectacular days, we also planned mini vacations within our vacation where we would take Mama Rich and Paw Paw along - that is when Paw Paw would go. One favorite spot was Noccalula Falls right near their hometown. It was a beautiful historic site on what was formerly known as Black Creek Falls. There was so much to do and see there; the cascading falls of course, but the quaint colonial town, the covered wood bridge, the nature trail, the playground, the campground and miniature golf. We would pack a picnic lunch, tour the falls, and then head towards the park and gardens for our picnic. There was nothing better than a day like that under the shaded old trees with the smell of Magnolias and Azaleas in the air and burgers cooking on grills.

One year however, we decided to take a longer trip to Six Flags. Atlanta was only a couple hours away so we geared up for the trip. Mama Rich was just as ready as us kids for this adventure. She was a woman who knew how to squeeze every ounce of joy out of life. After patiently enduring the more gentle attractions, the kids were itching for some excitement. Now what is more exciting than a roller coaster? My parents were less than thrilled about the possibilities, especially since it would've been too much for Mama Rich's heart and my mother's for that matter! A compromise was reached and we decided we would settle for the "Mining Train." It would be a nice easy ride along the tracks, through a few underground tunnels etc. Boy, were we wrong! This made the roller coaster look like a merry go round! That old mining train would dart in and out of dark caves narrowly missing railway posts and cavern walls. It wound up and down mountain trails and whipped sharply around the mountain's outer edge. I'll never forget the look on Mama Rich's face when we came to a stop. *We helped her to her feet. Her silver hair was tossed towards her face, and her glasses lay crooked on her nose like a wrecked bicycle. It took a while, but eventually that sweet, silly smile of hers cracked open her lips and then came that wide-open hearty laugh. I didn't want to admit it, but although I enjoyed the ride, I was also glad when it came to a stop.*

I suppose on life's ride nothing really "comes to a stop" unless it is the final destination. We will always face blind curves, dark tunnels and uphill climbs along the way. Sometimes though, my humanity gets the best of me and I just want things to stop, if but for a moment. Tonight is one of those nights. I stop to take a moment to find steady emotional ground to stand on and reach for something, somewhere to hold onto until the dizziness subsides. My heart feels so much love yet at the same time, so much fear, still, after all these years. My heart's ride has left me a bit shaken after deep hurt and divorce. Every so often, there is a sharp curve that knocks loose my "rose colored" glasses and I look in the mirror to see a rather disheveled mess! Why is it that the fairy tales never mention how much hard work love is? "Guard rails" do protect and defend my heart, but at times it seems they serve as a security gate - locking out the very things my heart longs for. I want to ride through life with total trust, faith and abandon, but sometimes, like tonight, all I can do is yell *"stop I want to get off!"* Is this the nature of a wounded heart? Up and down, in and out, round and round love goes...

Perhaps there is more. Perhaps the ups and downs aren't a mistake. Maybe they are a part of the grand design like a beautiful symphony or an intricate dance - highs, lows, moments of delight followed by somber moments of reflection and pause; each heart and life moving in and out, forward and back, not so much in a repetitive predictable motion, but rather fluttering like a butterfly, or whistling like the wind through the trees; maybe like the rays of sun peeking in and out of the clouds or the moon darting its head above and below a mountain peak. Perhaps this is love's true lesson that applies to every area of life. *"Perfect love drives at all fear."* This divine truth has escaped me for so long - longing to love yet at the same time so afraid; desiring to truly live, but settling for existence; daring to dream, yet shying away from the purpose placed deep in my heart.

I think rather than running in fear over the "unknown" trying to steady a hurting heart, it is time to let down the guard rails and allow love and life to be what they are meant to be, freely given, freely expressed, unfettered from impossible expectations and conditions, experienced with total confidence and assurance, embraced with quietness, strength, assurance and peaceful resolve. I have spent most of my adult life "preaching" a message of trust - for God, for family, for fellow man, for the process of life; yet trust escaped me in my own life. The truth is, it had escaped me because I had not learned to trust myself, my decisions, my instinct and that voice inside my beautiful heart that was a whisper from God's very heart. Instead of enjoying the ride of life and love as it was meant to be, I was shaky, fearful and ready to stop and never ride again. There was a huge lesson to be learned from that jolly gray-haired lady with the crooked smile on that little roller coaster that day. Mama Rich never once tried to stop the ride. When her oldest son took his own life, she kept moving forward loving her family, her community and trusting God and the process of life. When her only daughter had a massive stroke in her mid-fifties, this elderly mom loved her, cared for her, encouraged her and kept holding tight around life's curves. After her husband of sixty plus years was placed in a nursing home because she could not care for him at home, and then years later after his passing when she moved into a retirement home because she could no longer totally care for herself, she kept handling those up and down hills with a smile on her face, delight in her eyes and joy in her heart. I will never forget the last day I spoke to her to tell her how very much I loved her. She was ninety-four years old still encouraging me to keep going. Yes it is a ride, this thing we called life. Yes, there are ups and downs to the heart of life - this emotion we call love, but it is a ride worth experiencing with total trust.

CHAPTER 13

REFLECTION IN THE MIRROR

"In the beginning, this man said all the right words, had all the right answers but knew nothing about treating my heart and the love so deep within as a treasure. What began to unfold with this man, was the text book definition of mental and emotional abuse to a tee."

It is almost midnight but sleep is nowhere to be found. Strange as it may seem, I am too tired to sleep. As I glance over at the clock on my nightstand, the picture frame beside it captures my attention. I see words to a poem leaping out at me that were transposed on a photo. It is a poem that I wrote some time ago. The title of the poem is called "Reflection." The photo itself speaks volumes. It perhaps is even more descriptive than the words to the poem. In the eyes staring back at me I can see hurt, pain, longing and desire. Those familiar eyes from my past look so tired. I perfectly understand that look. I, too, get weary sometimes. We all do. Sometimes it is hard to let go of the past, embrace the present and soar into the future. I am still riding life's "roller coaster," and have come such a long way, but now I long for even more. I long for the wings of love to break free and soar. Actually, love is not the problem. As I've said before, I have a heart the size of Texas. No, it's that nagging monster of fear that is hiding in the bushes waiting to knock down anyone on a journey of love every time they start to spread their wings to fly. Fear - what a horrible creature! It can cripple the mind, stop the heart, and even change the color of your hair, so they say. One writer said, *"Fear has torment."* An understatement I feel. Coming from an abusive relationship, this monster has been even more daunting. Still, I know that somehow this enemy of my soul, this parasite that wants to suck out peace little by little will ultimately be conquered. I have knocked this creature down on many occasions and will continue to fight! Fear hides in the shadow of betrayal and divorce, of hurt and pain, and attempts to drain every ounce of peace possible. It lays waiting in the ditch of failure and lurks behind the tree of opportunity seeking to hinder us from relationships, from success, from promotions, from friendships, from prosperity and blessing, and from health and wholeness. Anytime a person pursues love and peace, anytime one sets out to accomplish a goal, to grow a relationship, or move forward in any aspect of life, it is most certain that "fear" will rear its ugly head trying to either drag you back into the past, or trip you up and knock you down in the present. Strangely though, as I face this villain of fear, I feel hope coursing through my veins in spite of the other emotions trying to saturate me. I know the answer. I've said it before and I will speak it until somehow, the message transforms me totally. *"Perfect love drives out all fear."* I am not totally there yet, but I have to believe I am on my way. I've come a long way in the last few years.

Three and a half years ago, I stood at a crossroads - not literally but figuratively. It was during the last stages of that most recent abusive relationship that I found myself in. I had opened my heart up to love one more time and love came back to haunt me. Not love, but the abuse of love. *In the beginning, this man said all the right words, had all the right answers but knew nothing about treating my heart and the love so deep within as a treasure. What began to unfold with this man, was the text book definition of mental and emotional abuse to a tee.* He had made every attempt to belittle me and to stifle the determination and tenacious spirit in me. He had controlled my every move for three years - telling me what I could and could not wear, where I could or could not go, accusing me of being unfaithful and deceitful, demeaning me in front of my family and friends. Worst of all, he had alienated me from them all - each and every voice of reason in my life. I had gauged my every thought and scrutinized every action I made as though even the mundane was a life and death decision. Perhaps it had been, because the mental and emotional control he had over me was debilitating; it was like slow death to me. I was not truly living, but only existing. He had masterfully invoked fear into every area of my life, while brainwashing me into believing that everything that happened was my doing and my fault. It was like déjà vu from the years I had spent in a dungeon of fear with my first husband. Once again, I was faced with a decision. Fear tried to threaten me into staying, but hope compelled me to leave. The crossroads of decision loomed in front of me. What a difficult place to be. It is certainly not for the faint at heart. We all face those crossroads on occasion, those points of no return where we have to commit one way or another.

When I was preparing for college, I was undecided on where I would attend. I was auditioning for a piano scholarship at two schools. I truly wanted to go where I was meant to be, so I prayed. *"God whichever school you want me to attend help me get a scholarship there."* So much for the prayer - I received a scholarship to both! The universe has a way of causing us to stretch the legs of faith and extend the arms of reason sometimes. I was standing before two open doors and had to choose. I was at a crossroads that would take me one direction or another never to return. Often, life is not all that cut and dry. Sometimes, it is meant for us to pray and meditate, use our insight, our wisdom and often just our gut instinct to make decisions, to make choices. We all pretty much know what is right and what is wrong and have that internal "gauge" that tells us so. Why is it we ignore it so often? I have been just as blind to my instincts at times as I am visually with my damaged sight.

When Josh was a little boy, he wanted what all little boys want - a BB gun. Now he did not get his wish the first go round, but finally showed himself responsible enough and wore me down enough that he got his first little gun. We had a blast with that BB gun! We would get out in the yard and shoot tin cans, tin pie plates, and paper plates - just about anything that resembled a target! I had become quite the markswoman through years of experience with my little brother's BB gun and target practicing with "real" guns at the shooting range with Josh's father. This time outdoors with Josh was a wonderful bonding time for the two of us. Although he knew better, Josh did what little boys do sometimes. He disobeyed! He slipped out into the yard by himself and started target practicing. This time however, he shot up into a tree. What a perfect shot - unfortunately. He nailed a little bird. The bird fell to the ground and Josh walked over to where he was. It was a heart-wrenching experience for him. No one told him it was wrong to kill, but his little heart knew. Somehow he just knew. Those "commandments" were written in his little heart. Yes, we all know, we all have that gut feeling on what is good and bad, right or wrong.

Lately my "gut" has been gnawing at me about something I've tried to ignore way too long. When will I ever learn to totally trust my heart? I've tried to use "peace" as my gauge through the years. It leads me when I am sensitive enough to listen. When there is an absence of peace, I know something is just not right. Looking at that "reflection" in the photo frame tonight, I understand. Fear robs peace. It had been ambushing me overtime for years. Sometimes it takes all the strength one can muster to fight the battle with this evil monster. It is so important not to allow Fear's roar drown out the whisper of our heart, or it's dark cloud cast a shadow on the face looking back at us in the mirror. From the time we were formed, we were given all that we need to discern what is right for our lives. Our bodies tell us when something is wrong, our emotions feel turmoil when something isn't quite right. Our hearts hurt when we are being treated in a way that does not serve our best interest. Our spirits grieve when things go awry. Peace truly is an internal weapon against fear. Through this divine resource, I have won many battles, but am not so naïve as to think the battle is over. It is a daily fight - but a fight I desire to win. The prize is something worth fighting for. As I find the resolve within to continue this battle on to victory, I feel a measure of peace flowing over me. I know I won't cut down the enemy of my heart with a sword, but must melt it with a torch - another weapon against fear - fervent love. This is the reflection that I have been longing to see, one of love that defies all odds.

CHAPTER 14

SHHH...

"I tried to speak but this precious brown-eyed boy that was so much a reflection of me stopped me. 'Shhh Mommy... be quiet, Jesus is trying to tell me something.' I felt a holy awe fill the room as I sat reverently on his bed. Who was I to doubt?"

Three years ago, I learned what a "job" the daily task of finding a job was. It was daunting and exhausting at times. By the end of the evening, I would finally shutdown the job link search engine and called it a night. My already crossed right eye would be doubled even more. A headache that seemed to be a permanent part of me would pound like a hammer over my eye. I understood all too well those career counselors who said that you should treat finding a job like having a job. It was definitely hard work! To wind down from the day one particular evening, I was listening to the sound of a spring rain. Well actually, it wasn't spring, and the "rain" was a synthetic sound on my "nature" machine. It was amazing how real it sounded when I closed my eyes. I was taken away to a quiet mountain retreat. I visualized a flowery meadow at the base of a snow-topped mountain. I looked out a screened porch as I listened to the sound of rain, while smelling the fresh air on a spring afternoon. It is truly amazing what we can visualize when we are still. It is in such moments like that when I can hear my own heartbeat in a multitude of ways. It is also in such moments that I find myself and I hear God's whisper in my ear.

When my son Josh was about four years old, we were living in a small town in Mississippi - a million miles from nowhere, it seemed. I had always been a "city girl," so I was out of my element, to say the least. I recall taking Josh to kindergarten there when he turned five. Each morning, we would head down those curvy country roads, make it past the hardware/grocery/deli/gas station and cross through the one street light to the little country elementary school. One afternoon, I was waiting with the other parents who were there to pick up their children. A burly older lady, with missing teeth and food stains on her blouse, was there to pick up her grandchild. She looked me over up and down and said *"You ain't from around here 'ere' ya?"* How could she tell? I was definitely a fish out of water. We ended up there after I had found the courage to give marriage another try. It was no surprise that I had been "gun shy" after being the recipient of a life of abuse with an addict. It had been ten years of triumph to torment, heaven to hell and everything in between. I vowed to never marry again. Oh… but there was that little voice ringing in my ear - that prayer that I could not ignore. Every night, from the time Josh was old enough to talk, he would plead with that innocent little voice *"Jesus, PLEASE bring me a new daddy."* My mistake was trying to help "Jesus" out a bit. Besides, marrying again was my way of saving myself from "myself" and how I had begun reaching out for what turned out to be more destructive, dead-end relationships. My life with this addict had started a pattern I had not wanted to fall into and desperately desired to stop in its tracks. I had not yet risen above, nor understood, what I was doing to myself and allowing others to do. I was living the life of a victim and not a victor. I was trying to fix something externally that was broken internally. There I was, married again, separated from family and friends in a small town where I had no one - feeling more alone than ever. Husband Number Two worked long hours. He left at three a.m. and returned around nine p.m. Exactly why were we married? It only took him two years to figure out he didn't have time for us. Between his long hours working and his previous family, children etc. he was stretched much too thin for yet another family. It wore him down until he became very ill and began pushing everyone away - his family included. Soon, Husband Number Two with tears in his eyes, asked us to leave. I confess, I had not been all that he needed. Hurt, loneliness and constantly feeling homesick began to build walls around my heart and shut down my emotions. Yes I was angry, but mostly angry at myself for making such a hasty decision. Hurt had bred more hurt it seemed - for both of us.

I was grateful for one thing during the short time we were there. Josh did not feel alone at all. He loved being in the country. What boy wouldn't? He had acres of wide open yard to tromp in, trees to climb, deer wandering in the back yard and a yellow lab named "Boomer" to keep him company. Oh and of course, he had a new "daddy" - at least part of the time. At night, I would go into Josh's room to tuck him in and say "nite-nite" prayers with him. He had quite the list for God each night. He prayed for every family member, every friend and acquaintance far and near. One night, I slipped in to pray with him. It appeared that he had started without me. *I tried to speak but this precious brown-eyed boy that was so much a reflection of me stopped me. "Shhh Mommy... be quiet, Jesus is trying to tell me something." I felt a holy awe fill the room as I sat reverently on his bed. Who was I to doubt?* After our prayer, I slipped quietly back to my own bed. My new husband lay there sound asleep from a long, exhausting day. As close as he was, I felt more alone than ever. I took a labored breath to choke back the tears. I wanted to speak, but felt as if I were being interrupted. *"Shhh, I want to tell you something."* For a moment, my heart was at peace and my mind at rest.

Tonight, I am experiencing one of those quiet reverent moments. In my mind, I hear the "sound of spring rain" soothing me and am visualizing a beautiful place. Actually, I don't have to visualize it so much. If I open my eyes and am very still, I can "see" it all around me. I have been brought to a divine place where "refreshing showers" through those I love have cleansed my heart and soul. I think about how far I've come in just a couple of years and how far I've come in a lifetime really. I've faced ups and downs and been exhausted at times and there have been voices around me shouting so loudly that I could not hear myself think. The truth is, as long as I am in this human body, the voices will never stop. They are forever pulling me in one direction or another each trying to win the battle for my soul and my peace of mind. It is just the way it is living in an imperfect world. Still, each time they try to distract me, I strain my ear to hear something stirring in the distance. Like the gentle melodic sound of "rain," a song plays in my head to quiet the noise and to whisper ever so lovingly in my heart...

The eyes of God are upon me,

He sees everything I do.

The arms of God are around me,

They keep me safe and secure.

And He knows where I am

Every hour of every day

He knows each thought I think

He knows each word that I might say.

And although there've been times

I've been out of His will

I've never been out of His care.

A little more each day, I feel the struggles from my past and cares of life slowly drifting away. My soul feels as if it is being rocked gently to sleep and again, I hear that familiar "whisper" in my heart... *"Shhh, I want to tell you something."*

CHAPTER 15

GOD WHISPERS AND ANGELS WINGS

"What he had to share made me go weak in the knees. He stated that at the very moment I sent him the message, he and a co-worker were walking together. Clint showed the message to his buddy. He looked up and one of the reactor tubes had broken. There was a piece of it dangling overhead. Had it fallen on anyone, it would've burned a hole completely through them."

Have you ever had a moment in your day when you just felt something or someone near? It was almost like a feathery brush against your skin or a whisper in your heart but you just knew that you weren't alone and that something invisible was taking place. These moments are a little different than the "shhh" moments when you are keenly aware of the voice of the Divine. They are more like a "sense" of something unseen. I've had these moments in my life. Maybe on a commute to or from work a car stalls in front of you or a detour is ahead, and when you finally get further down the road, you see that you just missed an accident by those few minutes delay. Perhaps you lose your keys or forget your textbook on the way to school, or your file folder on the way to a meeting and that delay causes you to arrive at just the right moment to sit near the very person you needed to interact with that day. I've had encounters with people in stores and various places that were nothing less than divine appointments. There is so much going on in the invisible. None of us truly know what all is being accomplished in what seems like nothingness to us. It could be in the form of your car skidding on a rainy highway avoiding an accident - stopping only inches from a guardrail like I experienced once; or perhaps first responders being "positioned" in a location prior to an accident or disaster seemingly by coincidence. Once when I was the victim of an automobile accident, after the impact, my truck skidded out of control across five lanes of traffic - missing all the cars, then swerved across a sidewalk narrowly missing pedestrians, an oak tree and a steel flagpole until finally, it crashed into a concrete and iron fence. My face hit the steering wheel - dazed, I desperately tried to get out of the truck. Once I pushed open the door and stood to my feet, blood began to pour from my battered face. Out of "nowhere" it seemed, two women appeared coming up the sidewalk. They began pulling pillows out of the back seat of my truck that we used on long trips - they laid them on the cold ground and gently placed me on top of the pillows, covering me with a blanket. *"It's okay sweetie, we are nurses. You're going to be okay."* Had they had a "God whisper" that day at lunch to walk that sidewalk at just that moment? Had "angel's wings" guided me across all that traffic, across that sidewalk of pedestrians and in between an oak tree and a flag pole? I am convinced of it.

My friend Clint works on a safety team at a chemical plant. His life and the life of others are literally in danger every day. Sometimes I'll send a message telling him to listen for his "angels." He has told me he is very aware of their presence each day because he has had a brush with death more than once both on and off the job. Hearing his stories reminds me of the stories we all read after the 911 disaster. There were so many people who were deterred from getting to work that day for one reason or another. I am convinced that "angels" were watching over them and that those things that some of them sensed were God whispers keeping them out of harm's way. Never underestimate the presence of the supernatural in your life. Never deny that the whole universe is orchestrated to guide and direct you when you have the ears to listen, the eyes to see and the heart to feel it. We all have these amazing encounters and experiences throughout our lives. Think about it for a moment. Perhaps you sense that you should go visit someone you haven't seen in awhile, or send an email to a friend with a certain motivational thought that you read that day. It could simply be a hunch about joining a contest, or putting a flashlight, blanket or jumper cables in the trunk of your car. Maybe it is just a "feeling" that you need to pick up the phone and check on a friend or family member. It could be a foreboding sense that something isn't quite right and you simply must express that concern to someone close to you. Now this does not mean we are exempt from disaster or suffering, but it does mean that sometimes if we are truly paying attention, we can avoid certain things headed towards us.

One of the most amazing "God whispers" came to my friend Laura. She came across a contest on the internet that was geared towards "transformation." It was a goal setting contest. She and I had been challenging each other for a couple of years, and so she thought joining the contest would motivate us both to push a bit harder to reach our goals and pursue our dreams. On a whim, I said *"sure why not?"* Within a month mind you, I had been given the opportunity to share a bit of my life story with forty-seven thousand contestants! Forty-seven thousand! Talk about a "God whisper." I had been pursuing open doors for many years, yet at the right moment, a "God whisper" ushered me into a vast global opportunity, changing my life forever. Another extremely powerful "God whisper" came to me a year and a half ago. Clint was working at the plant that day. I prayed for his angels as he also does daily. On into my work day, I came to a complete halt and began to cry. I just knew something was not right. I stopped and said a prayer for my friend. I wanted to dismiss it but I could not. I felt that strong tug inside and heard that "whisper" in my mind and heart. I messaged him and told him what I was feeling. I had no idea why I was saying what I did, but I told him that if he were walking on a ground level of the plant to be extra careful and to look up over his head. I said another prayer for him and then went about my day. Sometime later, I heard from him. *What he had to share made me go weak in the knees. He stated that at the very moment I sent him the message, he and a co-worker were walking together. Clint showed the message to his buddy. He looked up and one of the reactor tubes had broken. There was a piece of it dangling overhead. Had it fallen on anyone, it would've burned a hole completely through them.* They secured a safety net beneath it in case the piece fell and so this prevented anyone from walking underneath the reactor until it could be secured and replaced. "God whispers" are more real than your own voice! Never diminish the power of that voice inside. It may make the difference in a moment, a day or a life of someone.

Looking back over my experiences through years in an abusive marriage, I know that there were countless times that angels were watching over me - many times I knew about but even more that I was totally unaware of. I was in so many dangerous places - sometimes in my own home. One evening several years into my first marriage, my husband was late coming home from work - again. I had that foreboding "feeling" - that "whisper" that something was just not right. I sat in the recliner in our living room nervously rocking back and forth and quietly praying. As minutes and hours rolled on, I began to cry. I was worried about my husband and even more worried for myself. I never knew what I would deal with upon his return to the house. When he came in, I tried to remain calm and tried not to confront him in a way that would stir his irrational anger. This time, it took nothing more than my fearful tears to set him off. He pulled his 45 caliber pistol out of his pocket and began waving it around like a maniac. He screamed for me to shut up, but the more he screamed and waved his pistol, the harder my sobs became. I was hysterical. Before I knew what happened, a thunderous sound totally silenced my cries. The gun had been aimed and fired into the fireplace - brick and plaster exploded in a surreal display of the visual chaos I felt exploding inside my own mind and heart. I was afraid to breathe. Would I be his next target? Methodically he walked to the sofa, laid down with gun in hand and nodded off to sleep - passed out from his severe intoxicated state. The silence for those few moments in time was both smothering and serene. I quietly slipped out of the chair, walked to the sofa and eased the gun out of his dangling limp hand. I can't be certain, but I think I could hear the sound of angels wings that night. One thing I do know for sure is for a few moments frozen in time, I could "feel" them, gently holding me close, calming my fearful heart and bringing me peace. It's as if they had ushered me into the presence of God Himself and sat me safely in His lap, embraced by His caring arms.

CHAPTER 16

PAW PAW'S LAP

"That strong husky white-haired preacher man, with the big space between his front teeth, was like a big old cuddly bear. We would take turns as he grabbed two grandchildren at a time, and would place one on one knee and one on the other."

During a family reunion weekend sometime ago, I was out to dinner with some of my relatives. My cousin Rodney's grandchild was sitting across the table from me. He was about four or five, all boy and absolutely adorable. Those curious brown eyes and inquisitive nature reminded me of Josh at that age. Sitting next to him was my cousin Cathy. As we ate, Cooper paused with the most sincere and thoughtful expression on his face. *"Cat Cat, I was thinkin' 'bout somethin'."* *"You were?"* she asked. *"Yes, I was thinkin' that when I finished eating I could crawl up into your lap."* Oh that we had the honesty of a child when it came to what we were feeling, when it came to our needs and desires. As time goes on and we grow older, we shy away from that honesty, that vulnerability. I had expressed that very same thought a million times or more secretly in my mind and heart. When I didn't know if my preemie baby boy would live or die, my "mom face" showed strength, but the little girl in me longed for just a moment to be held and loved on. When I was packing up my belongings after divorce, illness and being forced to sell my home, I looked at my parents who were helping me move and wished I didn't have to hear how strong I needed to be, how I didn't need to be angry or how this was the "best thing." I longed to crawl up in their lap like I used to as a child, even if but for a moment.

When I was a little girl, my mom's dad, Paw Paw Weeks carried on a favorite tradition with us grandchildren. He had a little song he loved to sing. *That strong husky white-haired preacher man, with the big space between his front teeth, was like a big old cuddly bear. We would take turns as he grabbed two grandchildren at a time, and would place one on one knee and one on the other.* It was then he would chant. *"All I want in this creation is a pretty little wife and... two little boys to call me Pappy, one named Doc the other named Davy, one loves Sop the other loves Gravy. High diddly day."* What a safe, joyful place to be, bouncing around on Paw Paw's knee, sitting cradled in Paw Paw's lap! Years came and went as Paw Paw Weeks cradled grandchild after grandchild and then great grandchild after great grandchild in his lap. The last time I saw my Paw Paw was after he had a stroke and had been bedridden for years. He was just a shell of a man from that strong husky man from years ago. He had gone from the man holding up others physically and spiritually to the one being cradled in the arms of Maw Maw Weeks. How completely devoted she was! For years, she stopped all activity to sit by his bedside, feed him, dress him, talk to him, pray for him, stroke his confused brow, and still his hurting heart. She held him close and safe in her heart until the day, he went "home." At his funeral, my cousin Jason sang that spectacular song, *"I Can Only Imagine."* Paw Paw was no longer lying still in a bed teetering between this life and the life to come. He was dancing throughout the universe, singing with the angels a new joyful, playful song, being embraced by strong arms as he sat in the lap of God.

Several years ago after Paw Paw passed away, one evening the most ominous feeling came over me. I felt I had to pray and meditate - right then, right there! Before I knew it, my car seemed to be leading me straight to Maw Maw's house. She did not drive after dark, so I knew she would be home. I called her to make sure she was awake. The door opened and there my sweet grandmother stood, already in her pajamas dressed for bed, hair wrapped in her night scarf, and tears pouring down her face. She had been praying for me before I even arrived. We must've sat for an hour or more on her sofa, tears pouring down each of our faces, and my grandmother holding my hands in hers as she prayed, with all the faith in her soul. That day, my precious Maw Maw Weeks, with the faith of a saint, the love of God and the tenderness of a child allowed me to crawl into her lap. I've crawled up into her "lap" many times since then, and amazingly she has crawled into mine with the vulnerability of a child confessing how much she misses Paw Paw. She is always encouraging me not to sweat the small stuff but to grab life by the horns and enjoy every moment while I have the chance. *"Have a ball!"* she says… When I've forgotten who I am or lost sight of where I am going, she has reminded me cradling me in her arms of love.

There is something totally blissful about crawling up in someone's lap. When I was in college, a girlfriend and I were at the mall during the Christmas season. In the center of the mall was a big chair and a long line of children. You see, Santa was there and they were waiting for their special time to crawl up in Santa's lap. As I walked through the mall, "Santa" began to yell out *"Starla come see Santa, come sit in Santa's lap."* You can imagine my surprise. That child in me could not resist Santa's call and besides, I was curious to see who was behind that white beard and how he knew my name! As I sat on "Santa's" knee, I whispered *"who are you?"* As soon as I looked deep into his eyes and heard his voice, I recognized my friend Dale from school. What a lesson. We can be "lost in the crowd" with a need to be loved, nurtured and cared for and when we need it most, "love" finds a way to our heart and life, embracing, giving us a tender touch and a gentle reminder that we are not alone. Even when we try to appear strong, when we are too afraid to let down our guard, to be vulnerable, to express the deepest needs of our heart, love knows. Somehow love knows. I still have days and nights when I crawl up into "Paw Paw's" lap - well at least in my mind, heart, spirit and emotions. I feel the invisible arms of God wrapping me tight, holding me close; I feel the love of family and friends embracing me with random acts of kindness and words of appreciation, and even sense the touch of strangers through smiles and everyday courtesies and interaction. No matter what we've been through, what hurts we've carried, pains we've endured, grief we've walked through or loneliness we've experienced - no matter how fearful our steps in the dark have been or even our path in the light has been, love finds its way to us through most unexpected means. It has found its way into my darkest nights without a doubt, constantly reminding me that there is a safe place waiting for me somewhere each day through even the toughest of days - a place where I know that I am loved and I am not alone.

CHAPTER 17

JUST BECAUSE

"I lay in the stillness of the night, in pain, looking at that brown-eyed girl lost so long ago. I wondered if I had ever really been a child - the little girl in me seemed eternally lost in grown up expectations that I had taken on as early as I could remember."

Through a long job search a few years ago, among hundreds of applications that I filled out and sent in, I also completed an application for a job with the federal government. I'm sure many felt I was wasting my time since those jobs are so hard to come by. Quite frankly, I didn't really know if I was qualified or not, but I also felt that I would never know unless I gave it a shot. It is not always the most skilled athlete who wins the race, but the one who endures until he reaches the finish line. For so much of my life, I felt that everything that happened to me, everything good that came my way was because I earned it, because I performed my way into it and because I deserved it. By the same token, when something bad came my way, I felt it was because I had earned it in a negative way, through fear and lack of performance. When bad times came, I blamed myself and was left feeling very undeserving and unworthy. *"Perhaps if I had tried just a little harder... things would be different"* became my distorted thought process. Even when I saw evidence to the contrary, I still behaved like "Pavlov's Dog." Old habits die hard. Others would say *"jump"* and I would say *"how high?"* I simply could not see that difficulty came when I performed and difficulty came when I did not. There was obviously something more - something deeper than the externals. What wife deserves to be battered or what child deserves to be abused? What spouse deserves to be abandoned or hardworking person deserves to be laid off or become sick? Not everything is about performance. All of us, good and bad, are in an imperfect world and no one is exempt from suffering at times. We can however, readjust our mindset, our focus and our energy to move beyond constant negatives by the attitude we display through such times. Even through the worst of times, there is something valuable for us through them all. Perhaps it is a lesson to be learned, compassion to be displayed, character to be shaped and molded or tools and skills to be given and developed to help us along our journey forward. Combating life's pitfalls with a positive mindset and an acceptance and understanding of the process is the clearest way to rise above our circumstances. The blame game for others or even for ourselves keeps us stuck in the victim's world of existence. Sinking in negativity only draws more of it in our lives. It is so strange how we can be kind to perfect strangers and even those who we dislike or who hurt us, but we fall way short of being kind to ourselves...

Recently, I watched an interview of a famous actress. She is successful, wealthy, and beautiful. As she began to tell her "story," I realized again that not everything is based on what we do or how well we do it. Sometimes no matter what - "life" just isn't fair. This lady had come from an abusive home as a child and she battled low self-esteem her whole life. Every choice she made, every goal she aspired to had been based in direct response to that fractured girl that lived inside her heart. She ended up in an abusive marriage, being beaten down not just physically but emotionally. Hearing her story and reliving mine along with hers, wove that "common thread" so many like us share. Low self-esteem is a thief and a robber of one's life. When someone's self-esteem is shattered, it really doesn't matter how much one does, acquires or achieves, nothing fills the emptiness inside. Every choice in life is a feeble attempt to fill that void. The truth be told, it is the over-achievers in this world who can often have the emptiest hearts inside. For a person with low self-esteem it is both a struggle and a journey to finally realize that you are worthy to be loved, and to find the courage to give and receive love. For me, I have seen "footprints" in my heart where Divine Love so lovingly and patiently walked and gently danced until the light of truth filled my deepest longings. Now, I find a quiet place where I am at rest. There is no human touch that can replace my Maker's arms holding me close and no human voice that can speak peace like God's gentle whisper.

Eleven years ago after "Husband Number Two," I found myself circling in the wilderness looking for the Promised Land again. Surprisingly, things improved much sooner than I anticipated and I actually began to smile and to look forward to my days once again. Josh and I were back at home close to family and he had adjusted beautifully; I had acquired a stable job and had bought a home all on my own. We were a family - even without a dad. How I wished I had learned that lesson a few years before. Home and family come in all sizes and shapes. You know what they say about hindsight. After about a year in our home, my "stable" job dried up. Through it all however, peace remained and in a very few months, I had another job opportunity - even better than before. I was back out on life's "stage" again, performing better than ever. I was too busy to realize that my peace was slowly, but surely slipping away once more. The more I had, the lonelier I felt; the more stability I acquired, the emptier I became. I had crammed so much in that empty place in my life that I was on the verge of imploding. At one point, I was working as much as ninety hours in a week, in addition to four or more choral rehearsals a week and teaching a weekly class. I was "meeting myself" at the door, so it seemed. Also, though I had vowed to never date again, I had allowed someone into my life and was wading through another relationship. I thought "love" deserved one more chance. Amazingly enough with this new man in my life, "love" did come, but it was between two broken hearted people with holes in their hearts. We were just temporary substitutes for what we truly needed and longed for. I am amazed at how many people are out there moving from person to person, in and out of relationships, breeding hurt and more hurt; desperately trying to fill that void inside - myself included for so long. During this time of my life, I had become my own worst enemy thinking that I had "arrived." I jumped back up onto that stage that had haunted me since childhood.

Stress is truly the silent killer. It wrapped its arms around me and began to squeeze the life out of me little by little. I found myself tired... not just mentally, emotionally or spiritually, but physically - I was exhausted. That monster of illness that had plagued me my whole life was sneaking up on me, yet again. I would wake up in the morning tired and go to bed tired. Then came the pain, intermittently at first, but then it took up residence like an unwelcomed guest. After sixteen months, the migraine on the right side of my head still refused to ease up. It worsened day by day until my wounded right eye completely crossed from the pain. Before I knew what happened, I was completely incapacitated. The familiar, yet foreboding face of darkness stared me in the eye piercing to my very soul. As I sat staring back at this emotional monster, a blanket of despair covered me like a coffin. Everything that I had been, done and known seemed dead. Another chance at life had slipped through my fingers. I was in constant fear of losing my job and even more, losing my life. Sickness pervaded my body like a marching army of ants and questions bombarded my mind. What could I do now? I had become so weak that a day's work was monumental; caring for my child and home were daunting. I was so debilitated that Josh, at age ten, was taking care of things around the house - making sandwiches, pouring glasses of tea, bringing me water, cleaning the kitchen and bathrooms, gathering and folding laundry, waking me up from the sofa and helping me make my way to bed. He would make sure the doors were locked each night and would turn off the lights. He had become the "adult." I was only able to get out of bed for an hour at a time before fatigue overwhelmed me. I was now a size "2" and had dwindled down to nothing - physically and emotionally. All the things I loved to do and the contributions I longed to make were at a standstill. After all of this time and all the lessons I should've learned, life was still about the "doing" - on my job, volunteering at my church, and being the family member everyone counted on. That little "Starla" had learned this early on. Why was it so hard for me to see the light? Everything I was seemed to be about what I did and how well I did it; always doing something to find value and worth and not seeing any in the stillness - only in the activity. The apple had not fallen very far from my mom's tree, it seemed. *I lay in the stillness of the night, in pain, looking at that brown-eyed girl lost so long ago. I wondered if I had ever really been a child - the little girl in me seemed eternally lost in grown up expectations that I had taken on as early as I could remember.* It is amazing how many children take on grown up expectations for one reason or another. Sometimes it is due to low self-esteem or the illness or absence of a parent. How often will the child of a sick mom or dad step up and become the adult like my little Josh did? Or a son will become the "man" of the house when Daddy leaves, or shoulder the responsibility of mom's protector if Dad is abusive? One never truly knows how early life experiences affect and alter a person all throughout their life. Concerning my own burdens from those grown up expectations, I honestly don't know exactly when or why I began to take on their heavy load. Looking back, I couldn't really say if they were imposed on me or if I took them on willingly, but either way it happened, and I had developed a lifetime pattern of associating my activity with my worth. It was no wonder that I felt so useless now as an adult who could not perform on my job, take care of my child, sing in my church choir or teach classes and lead community groups. What good was I now? I sat in the silence of the night as tears stained my cheeks. Each teardrop reminded me of that broken young woman who sat atop that platform looking out over the "zip line." Like that woman those years ago, again I was tired... so very tired. As I cried into the night, that feeling of hopelessness and uselessness, that had haunted me more times than I could count, swept over me again.

I had almost forgotten what that "whisper" sounded like, but in a most unexpected moment, my feelings of despair gave way to a tiny light piercing the darkness. As it permeated the room, hope beamed again like that beacon in the night. What had seemed like a dungeon before had become a place of refuge. I found that place of refuge through the light of my own soul. It illuminated a path straight to my heart. It was at that moment, I was once again reminded that I was not alone. As I sat in the stillness of my "night," that beacon of light dispelled a darkness that was filled with everything I had known, been and done. For the first time, I saw things not in the light of performance or expectations, but in the light of love. A voice, stronger yet more gentle than I can adequately describe, spoke to me bringing warmth and comfort that I had long since forgotten. The words still play like beautiful music in the recesses of my heart. *"You are loved. Not because of what you do or who you are, but just because..."* Finally "Someone" did not need my "stuff," my doing, but simply my "being" - "Someone" wanted me! I had been aware of that "Someone" in my life since I was a small girl, but it wasn't until that night, that moment, that I truly understood the depths of His love. I had spent all those years walking along the perimeters, but not fully diving in to all that this love had to offer. I began a new leg to my journey that night that would lead to places I had never been or known. Like the day of the zip line, my heart felt free. My desire was to never again to succumb to a love less than that of the Divine. Unlike others, God desired to lavish His love on me, just because...

CHAPTER 18

REVOLVING DOOR

"How could a woman so in tune with the love of God, of the Divine, have allowed so many people to circle through her heart so carelessly? I gave my heart to anyone who would invest a little time for it."

Have you ever been in a high rise of some sort whose entrance is a revolving door? If you have a little luck and skill you can enter that building without being pushed right back out. Still though, once you are inside, you are in an open lobby on the outer edge of where you need to be. The rooms or offices are closed off and require special access to enter. As I reflect back on much of my life, I think my heart had been guarded by a revolving "door." I allowed some people to come inside the lobby, sent others spinning right back out onto the street and allowed virtually no one into ALL the rooms of my heart - sadly, not even God. There were things that I was too hesitant for even my Maker to see. I struggled for many years with fully grasping divine unconditional love, especially if it came in the form of human hands and hearts. As a teen, I never wanted my school mates to see how different I felt through the burden of expectations that I simply could not understand. By the same token, I did not want to let my loving parents down as they were the one's I felt I needed to meet those expectations for - so I closed off doors to my heart... even to them. I didn't want them to know the hurt and confusion that was hidden inside. They would not understand how I felt missing special class parties, homecomings and proms a few times a year for commitments at our church or with family. There were more questions than answers and it was just easier to pretend that everything was okay. So I smiled, and obeyed and cried when no one was looking. Yes, I closed certain doors and refused total access to the rooms of my heart to anyone. I let them all in, but just so far. No one would see all that was hidden in the deepest rooms of my heart.

When Josh started kindergarten, I determined I was going to be the perfect mom. I kept a stiff upper lip and refused to cry each day. I packed a lunch with all of his favorites. I gave him money each day for snack time during their daily visits to the vending machines for one special treat. One afternoon, Josh came home talking ninety to nothing! He had always been blessed with the "gift of gab" and like all other Rich's, came by it naturally. This day however, he was "speed talking." As he talked, he began circling the floor, going round and round, faster and faster. He would run across the room and was almost bouncing off the walls. I knew something was not quite right. Patiently and carefully, I began to ask my little one about his day - what he did, if he ate his lunch etc. Then I asked him if he bought a treat during snack time. Well of course he did, boys would never give up the chance for a snack - at least not my boy. I asked him what he had. *"Mommy I got a 'Surge' drink from the machine."* I was livid! How dare they offer a drink with that much caffeine content to pre-schoolers! I held back nothing in voicing my disapproval to the teacher the next day. Joshua's erratic behavior that day reminds me of how similar our treatment of relationships is sometimes - at least mine had been. Relationships in our lives are the essence of true living as none of us are meant to walk through life alone. We need family, friends, companions, neighbors... However, when a relationship is broken or damaged, a person's objectivity and relational skills suffer. Whether we are running from hurt or trying to cover it, we can find ourselves reaching for something that is totally unfamiliar, like that caffeine drink was for Josh that day. We, too, begin spinning round and round, trying to find the right access to another's heart or to allow access to our heart. Strangely, those around us can see just how out of control we are, but in the newness of the moment, we are oblivious. It can become like a game of tug of war, pulling near and letting go, back and forth, up and down like a yo-yo… longing to hold that special someone close, but sometimes allowing fear and hurt to push them away just as quickly as they open up and draw near with a loving heart. Emotional baggage can cause one to do the very things you do not desire to do, and to push away the very one's you need and long for most. To those of you who have "been there," I am certain you can relate. To those of you who have been the recipient of such behavior from a person who has been hurt in someway through their relationships, perhaps it brings clarity and understanding, and maybe even compassion for the behavior. It can be heart wrenching to open up and trust and to move close emotionally only to be pushed away time and time again, due to fear. I have seen this pattern with so many over the years, who have battled fear due to painful relationship issues. The concept of loving and being loved "just because" is hard to grasp when you haven't displayed this kind of love to yourself. This is why it is so vital to develop healthy self-love and to properly heal from past hurts before stepping into new relationships of any kind really.

I reflect on my own relationships. With each door that I closed, they closed… each door they closed, I closed. Looking at the revolving door of my heart, I have to confess. No one person is to blame. We all make mistakes that causes hurt, at one point or another. There is no such thing as a "no fault" divorce or break-up. Each person is partially at fault and must take responsibility for their actions. There is no such thing as a "no fault" falling out in friendships or family matters either. Maybe one displays wrongs actions while another displays wrong re-actions, but the point is, we can only be responsible for one person - ourselves. Otherwise, we continue to harbor hurt and live the life of a victim. It has taken a long time for me to understand my mistakes, my failures and to take responsibility for the way I drew others in with a loving heart but then allowed fear and hurt to shut the doors and send them spinning back out. Everyone has closed heart doors of some sort, I suppose, in various types of relationships - be it with a companion, friend, family, co-worker, neighbor etc. These doors are like walls defending us from hurt and pain, but also can cause that very thing. Now, looking back on these relationships in my past, I wonder. Why have I searched so long for someone to fill empty rooms in my heart only to lock them out? *How could a woman so in tune with the love of God, of the Divine, have allowed so many people to circle through her heart so carelessly? I gave my heart to anyone who would invest a little time for it.* After years of spousal abuse, I no longer felt worthy of anyone's love, so I opened my heart to everyone in hopes that someone would love me, truly love me... I gave and loved, encouraged and built up, pumped up, fluffed up and accepted EVERYTHING. My gift of encouragement became distorted, warped and manipulated as I gave all of my best to those who could not or would not receive or appreciate all the love I had to offer. I gave everyone my best except "me." Sometimes those who are very loving, open and giving, allow emotional misuse not understanding that even love must have healthy boundaries. In reality, failure to do so, pushes a would be companion away! If you do not treasure "you," how can you expect him or her to? A friend of mine calls these types of relationships "missionary dating." That simply means you give all you have to give to another person to better their life and help them be a better person and rather than giving you that same type of love and encouragement, they take what they have gained into a new relationship and are a better person for the next partner! I think I had more than mastered "missionary dating!" I couldn't blame others really, because I had allowed it. I had not set boundaries on what I would or would not accept, what I needed and desired. How empty I felt time and time again. Even before the abuse those many years ago, I had felt insecure - unworthy. This was why I had settled in my first marriage to begin with. This is why it is so important to be completely at home in your own heart, to make sure you have explored every room of your heart. This is also why it is imperative to foster a healthy mindset and perception of self and to be pursuing a life that is uniquely your own where you are living every moment with authenticity. When you are walking in complete love and acceptance of yourself, you are better able to spot the signs of a charlatan or, at the least, another broken heart who is also insecure and not ready for love. There are signs and there are red flags, but an insecure person, a person with an empty love tank often mistakes these signs for opportunities to show their worth by displaying unconditional love. No one has been given the role of "savior" in a relationship. That is God's job!

As for my own insecurity and feeling of unworthiness - I still ask myself what it was that produced this empty longing in my past. Perhaps I would never know. My heart had revolved like that door, circling people in and out, in and out. Circle is an apt description. I simply was unable to allow others full access as long as I kept doors shut to even myself. There was always at least one room that I kept tightly shut. You know that place - where we must face all of our fears, hurts, unmet expectations and desires, personal failures and frailties and everything in between. It is a room that we often do not even allow our Creator to enter. While it is important to guard your heart, hurts can cause you to close off your heart a room at a time, shutting others out and locking you in before you realize it. It takes courage to open one's heart with no reserve. As I am finding more courage to open up, I must ask myself hard questions. What is it that I have been so afraid of? Them? Me?

The night is quiet. Everyone in my house is still, if but for a moment. I do hear a noise, however. It sounds like a tap. Is that someone knocking at my door? Fear and excitement are wrestling around in my heart. *"Open the door."* Someone whispers. *"No! You mustn't let Him in!"* screams the other. Still, He knocks. I hear His voice outside my door. *"Starla, I love you. I love you… I LOVE YOU!"* Unlike many others, His words are not hollow. He's proved it time and time again; and still, I've shut Him out at times! He has used every way imaginable to shower His love on me and show me He loves me - yes "just because." Longing fills my heart and that same peace that covers me each night wraps me up again.

RUNNING IN CIRCLES

"Dad was normally very docile by nature, but this had pushed him to his limit. He jumped up from his chair, picked up the wounded one and pitched it against the back door. More pieces flew. I wanted to laugh but didn't dare."

Sometime ago we were taking a walk through the neighborhood. Along the way, a frisky little dog joined our company. He had been playing in a yard with some children and then meandered along behind us as we walked. Sometimes he would go in front of us, cross the street beside us or trail a ways back. He was definitely vying for our attention but pretending to ignore us. What he did was the strangest thing I had ever seen. He would pick out the best mailboxes to "make his mark." He would lift that little leg of his and let it go. As we observed him, he would stop at mailbox after mailbox and "do his thing." Now I was certain at some point in time, that no matter how much water he had consumed earlier that day, he would have to run dry. Still he would "lift and aim, marking his territory." The funny thing about his behavior was how selective he was in his choices. If a mailbox was not one of those fancy brick ones and appeared rather ordinary, he would skip past it, run around us in circles and then move on to his next spot. He was running in circles to get our attention, but then ignoring us once we offered it.

When my brother Craig and I were children, my dad had to work long hours. He was a machinist and for awhile he worked shift work and would be gone in the evenings. He also was the Sunday School Superintendent at the church, so he was always quite busy. Sometimes it seemed that my brother Craig was like that little dog - running in circles from one place to the next trying to get Daddy's attention. Once, he ran to the bathroom closet, took out the plunger and jumped up on the dining room table and stuck it right in the bowl of potato salad that my mother had taken so much time and effort to make. When he was even younger, he wrapped himself in mom's most expensive living room curtains along with his dirty diaper. What an awful mess! Another evening in later years, Craig got a bit over-exuberant watching his favorite western on TV. Before Dad and Craig knew what happened, my brother picked up his BB gun, aimed it at the picture tube and fired. Thank goodness it only chipped the glass and didn't penetrate. What an explosion that would've made! My brother was all boy!

As Craig got a little older, he developed that annoying "boy" habit of leaning back in chairs at the dining room table. I recall one evening vividly. Once again, he was leaning back in the chair after Dad had told him not to for the thousandth time. This time, the chair kept on leaning - straight back to the ground after one of the legs broke. *"I told you not to lean back in the chair!"* My dad shouted. **Dad was normally very docile by nature, but this had pushed him to his limit. He jumped up from his chair, picked up the wounded one and pitched it against the back door. More pieces flew. I wanted to laugh but didn't dare.** *"Now then, you won't lean back in it again will you?!"* No of course not; there was nothing left to lean back in! My dad was a fair man, but if you pushed his buttons one too many times, you knew you had made a mistake. Daddy hated one thing worst of all. He hated to invoke punishment for something we had done. He left the "spankings" mostly up to my mom. Now perhaps you didn't receive "spankings" or possibly do not believe in them, but I am most grateful for them. My parents cared enough to teach us right from wrong. Often, it was more of a "talking to" than an actual "lick on the backside" and was always given with much love and care. I usually took them pretty courageously because I knew if I didn't whine or run away the severity would be much less. My brother just never could grasp that concept, however. I still can see my dad with his looped belt in one hand, and his other hand grabbing for Craig as my brother ran round and round in circles trying to avoid the sting of the belt on his backside. It was a sight to see. Dad would always say something that never made sense to me - *"This hurts me more than it hurts you."* Yeah right. Afterwards, Dad did something that was more painful than the spanking itself. He would hold us close, tell us to crawl up in his lap and tell him we loved him. This was so hard! The spanking was a piece of cake compared to this. Yet each time, the tears would come, our hearts would melt and Daddy would hold us close.

The concept of "spanking" didn't work well for my son. Josh was good hearted and well-behaved, but he had his strong-willed moments like every other child. When he was just a toddler, we would "spank" his hand as he would go to grab something that was breakable or off limits for him. He went through a phase, however, where this was not much of a deterrent. If he had it in his head to do something, he would simply hold out his hand and say *"pank me Mama.,"* which was his way of saying *"I am going to do it anyway, so might as well get the punishment out of the way!"* For the most part however, just talking to him and expressing disappointment over his behavior was a strong deterrent. He would usually come to me and tell me he had done something wrong even before I confronted him. Seeing the disappointment in my eyes and hearing it in my voice, broke his little heart. The tears would flow and the lesson would be learned in a much gentler way. Most of all, he knew just how much he was loved.

Well as for Daddy... he was not a very affectionate man by nature, but he was one of the most caring men I knew. He worked long and hard hours to provide for his family and then always found time to play with us in the yard, to watch a favorite TV program, or simply allow us to talk about our day. If something needed doing, Daddy would do it. If he didn't know how to do it, he would figure it out. In the eyes of a little girl, he was the smartest man I knew! When I was only twelve, my mom went back to work at a public job. Since he got off work sooner than she did, Dad and I would find our way to the kitchen and would prepare supper for the family. I wouldn't trade these moments for all the gold in Ft. Knox. I realize how often I took his love, provision, protection and correction for granted. I suppose that is something I've continued to do both with him and with my spiritual "Daddy" at times. How many days I've wasted "running in circles" like my brother did. How I wish I had found the courage to receive God's help and strength to right what was wrong in my life. If I had fully allowed those much needed lessons, I would have gained so much more, much sooner. By running from my own hurt I was hurting the One who loves me most, even more. Still, He pursued me, loved me and never let me go. One of my favorite songs is by the group Rascal Flatts that says "I Won't Let Go." This is my Creator's promise to me, to each one of us. Sometimes He fulfills it through the love of one person who is always there and that we can depend on and trust. I have found that to be true. There have been a few people in my life who have stood by my side no matter what. Even when I could not fully express my love to them or care for them as I should, they have been right there. There have also been people that I have loved in that same manner - people who have closed their heart's off afraid to love, afraid to open the door and let someone totally in, yet I would let them know through my friendship and devotion that I was there and *"I won't let go."*

I have a friend in South Africa named Frank. Frank and I "met" through a transformation contest that we both signed up for. My friend is a professional day trader and recently, he talked about a moment in his day when he was doing his market analysis and calculating his project run. In the course of his normal process, the electricity went down for an hour. Normally, he would've closed early because he would get nervous, but because of the time that had elapsed, he could not control his trade exit. He simply had to make the move. To his delight, it was much better than he could've imagined or that would've been had he followed his normal pattern of closing a bit early. His return was actually double! He was ecstatic realizing that this was a divine moment for him. His exact words were *"Don't ever doubt that the Divine way is not the best road to travel. Just get your human self out of the way of great things waiting to manifest in your life."* We spend so much of our lives running in circles, fighting the very people and things that are good for us and meant to be great blessing in our lives. As I think of how I have run in circles, run away from the love of others, run away from my hurt and from God's correction and care, I imagine Him looking down with tear-stained eyes each time I would stumble and fall, each time my heart would pull away from Him and end up broken. I think He, too, was saying like my dad used to say when he would correct us, *"This hurts me more than it does you."* As a parent myself, I totally understand that. Seeing your child hurt or straying from what is good or best for them is more hurtful than words can express. Nothing warms the heart of a parent like cradling your child in your arms, soothing their hurts. We do not have to run in circles in life. There is a place of refuge. The love of our Maker offers a road back no matter how far away from home we feel. His divine arms are always open ready and waiting for us to crawl up in His lap once again.

CHAPTER 20

WHO ARE YOU?

"Again, I was running in circles and jumping through hoops to try to find acceptance and each time I did, I lost a little more of myself and the way back seemed harder to find."

The other day I was running an errand for my mom. After arriving at the grocery store, I had a question about a certain item. I called her to ask about it, but unfortunately, my dad answered the phone. I say unfortunate because he is very hard of hearing and was not wearing his hearing aids. My dad was asking who I was and what I needed as though I were a complete stranger! In an odd sort of way, I could relate. There had been times of my life when I had been so filled with hurt, anger, fear and insecurities, that things I had said and done were totally foreign to that lovely girl hiding deep inside and I was left wondering who this person was. It is hard to believe how far away a person can feel from their own heart during life's most painful moments.

I was at a family gathering once when an uncle of mine who loves psychology and will take every opportunity to practice its concepts, came up to me and asked *"who are you?"* Of course I teasingly answered *"Starla."* He was not deterred. He replied *"truly though, who are you inside?"* I suppose there are times we all ask ourselves that same question. That has not been my only question throughout life. Sometimes it isn't so much a struggle determining "who I am" as much as "where I am." We all feel lost at one time or another.

Several years ago, my cousin Cathy and I were heading out to the mall. The day turned out to be one of those typical southern summer days, complete with a summer downpour. I met her at a nearby bank to leave my car and ride with her. The rain was torrential! Cathy parked on my driver's side and I slipped out the door and hopped into her car. About an hour into our excursion, my cell phone rang. It was Dad. *"Where are you?"* he asked. He proceeded to tell me that he had received a call from Ms. Sally a lady from my church who worked at the bank. She said that the bank security guard had reported a car parked in the bank's lot that was running with no one in it. She recognized the car - it was mine! The sound of the rain had been so loud, and I was in such a rush not to get drenched, that I had left the keys in my car, locked the door and left the car running.

My poor dad. He must feel as if he is in a constant state of confusion wondering who I am and where I am! Thank goodness my supernatural "Father" always knows who I am when I call on Him and He knows where I am every moment of the day as He watches over me. A familiar song rings in my ear again, *"He knows where I am every hour of every day; He knows each thought I think, He knows each word that I might say…"* There have been times in my life where I behaved emotionally just like I did with my car that day in the rain. I had tried desperately to get where I was going without getting drenched by the downpour of life, only to leave behind something of great value with its power and resources draining away. All the while, I had been totally unaware.

One of the most recent times occurred a few years ago. Things in my life had become so out of balance that I felt like I did that day in the rain. I just wanted to hop in a car and run before problems, fears and hurts turned into the perfect storm threatening to drench me. All the progression I had made since my divorce and health issues were slowly undermined through a relationship with someone from my past. This person had been a friend in my teen years, yet when we renewed the friendship, I was completely blindsided and found myself traveling down a dark road that was taking me further away from "home" and further away from "me." *Again, I was running in circles and jumping through hoops to try to find acceptance and each time I did, I lost a little more of myself and the way back seemed harder to find.* Before I knew what had happened, I was isolated from family and friends and totally absorbed in the one person who said he wanted to be my anchor and safe harbor. After all these years, I was still so trusting, still so naïve. I accepted him with the pure heart of that teenage girl so long ago, not taking the time to use the wisdom I had gained over the years. I saw him through the eyes of a fifteen year old, not an emotionally healthy woman. Had I been thinking clearly, I would've recognized the signs. Goodness knows I had many "red flags" waved in my face over the years - more than enough to know. I think in a strange way, I was trying to relive the missed days of my youth and wipe out all the hurt and pain since that time. So I fell head long into distorted memories of the past with my "high school crush," believing that in him I would find a refuge. What I had yet to realize, was that I already had an anchor, a safe harbor. My family and circle of friends had been that for me time and time again. They had been God's heart and embrace to me. But again, I found myself pulling away from them. Oh I was saying all the right words, smiling on the outside, walking with an air of confidence, and striving to be the perfect family girl, the church girl, the daughter, the friend, the mother, but on the inside I was shaking, fearful, lonely and hurting. I wondered how long it would take for those around me to see that I struggled doing a decent job in any of the roles of my life. There was a part of me that still did not feel worthy of their love and acceptance, their steadfastness and care. After all these years since my first marriage, there was still so much hurt and fear hidden away in my heart. I had allowed sixteen years of "busyness" cover the pain in my heart without truly dealing with it -

sweeping it under the rug which only compounded it. The only thing I knew to do to avoid its pain was to run - again. So, I took a "sabbatical" of sorts. I walked away from certain responsibilities that I felt were weighing me down and zapping my energy and focus. The thing that was truly zapping my energy and focus wasn't those things and activities, but a constant battle in my heart and soul, between my hurting heart and a committed spirit. Once again, the hurting heart won. I resigned my positions at church, took a job near the man I was dating and told some of my closest friends and family that I needed some "me" time to change direction. Stepping away from people whom I had been so close to and loved dearly made me feel as if a part of me had "died." I suppose it had, because truthfully, I wasn't stepping away from them, I was stepping away from "me" and trying to become something that I wasn't all because of that insatiable need for love and acceptance. I told myself that this was a good thing - I was retreating in order to come to terms with things that I had buried deep inside for years and convinced myself that it required standing on my own two feet apart from those who loved and supported me. I still did not understand the importance of opening myself up to those I loved with totally honesty about my fears, hurts and failures. I had not learned to face myself, so facing them was daunting. I could not admit that it wasn't a "retreat" but more of that game of "hide and seek" that I had played with myself for years. Yes, I convinced myself and others that I needed solitude time. How I wish I had known that it was the last thing I needed! How I wish that I had realized that I was not standing on my own two feet at all. I was following the pied piper of loneliness and hurt hoping that this time - this man would be the one that would accept me. Before I knew what happened, I found myself in another unhealthy relationship more alone, lost and afraid than ever. I still was "looking for love" in all the "wrong places," people and things. Like the day I climbed thirty feet to "find myself" on the zip line, I had traveled miles away from home to find "home" again - to find "me" again.

For three long years, I traveled on this quest for "self." What I was searching for was as close as my heartbeat, as gentle as the divine whisper in my soul. Like the "prodigal," the reason that I left became the same reason I came home. When I did, no one had to ask "who are you?" I no longer had to ask who I was either. I was the same lovely woman I had always been; the heart of the same precious brown-eyed girl still resided deep within this woman's hurting and battered heart. Through the words of a kindred spirit who believed in me and through the open arms and hearts of my family and friends I found a bridge back home...

CHAPTER 21

A MILE IN MY BOOTS

"They surrounded us and our vehicle like a gang on a playground. I must admit, I was taken aback and quite shocked. The insults that came afterwards spoke of my 'southern' accent, my crossed eye, my 'old lady' physique, my short hair and my broken past. This 'square peg' did not fit into their round hole!"

A few years ago, I had the opportunity to watch a movie that had been out for awhile but I never took the opportunity to see. In it, Sandra Bullock played a wacky brainiac who created crossword puzzles for a living. She was quite intelligent, but lacked in every day social skills. As the plot unfolds, the character embarks on a quest to find "normal" realizing that "normal" is all relative. She is looking for love and finds that it was inside of her all along. She is a very unique person, totally misunderstood, yet seeking desperately to be understood and accepted. As she marched across the country in her red go go boots speaking of the crossword puzzles of "life" and longing for someone to notice her, she exemplified the proverbial "square peg in a round hole." What she and everyone else ultimately sees, is that she is perfect just the way she is, in all of her uniqueness. I must confess, I shed a few tears as my heart found common ground with this quirky, yet special, woman. I, too, had been marching through life in my own set of "red go go boots." Who was it anyway that set the standard for "normal?"

When I was in college, I had a friend who had come to college a few years later than most. He really wasn't there for an education, but was on a quest. He had endured a painful divorce after a destructive time in his life and came to the college to pursue his ex-wife who was enrolled there. He was determined to show her he had changed in hopes to win her heart again. He was not your average "Joe." Our college was in the hills of Tennessee, and although we had a very diverse student population, "southerners" were the majority. Hank was anything but a southerner. He was a bleach blonde, hazel-eyed West Coast boy that wore flip-flops even on a snowy Tennessee day. He cruised through campus in his fancy car flashing his self-absorbing smile that masked the pain deep in his heart. Our first encounter was when he came barreling through campus speeding through the pedestrians crossing, honking his horn and yelling at me for being in the road. Of course, I yelled back at him for not yielding to pedestrians. How arrogant he seemed! He and I were exact opposites of each other, but it seemed we shared a kindred spirit in ways that were hard to explain. I understood his need for validation and affirmation, and even his childish antics to be noticed. Mine were more "mature" in nature, but in my own way, I seemed to be crying out for someone to truly "see" me. During the course of Hank's college experience, he began to soften. He met people who looked past that cocky demeanor, past the mistakes he had made in his marriage and with his life, past his current struggles and shortcomings and who saw a wounded heart that was in need of healing and restoral. That tough outer shell was simply masking a vulnerable heart. Receiving love and friendship from others who took the time to chip away at that outer shell seemed to open his heart to love, giving him hope for restoral of his life and marriage.

The fall could be quite cold in those Tennessee hills. One day, Hank was adamant that he had to have answers. He wanted God to hear his prayers and bring his beautiful vivacious brown-haired wife back to him. He asked me and his roommate to carry him to the mountains. He was going to camp near Lake Chilhowee until he *"heard from God."* He took only a tent, a bedroll and his Bible. He vowed not to eat or drink until something happened. We all tried to talk him out of it, but he was one of a kind and he was determined. He definitely did not follow the pack. We left our stubborn friend on a cold Tennessee night, with only the soft glow of the moon breaking up the dark eerie sky as owls hooted and imagination lurked behind every tree. The next afternoon, we received a phone call from a pay phone a few miles outside of the lake campsite. Not to my surprise, it was Hank. *"I've heard all I need to hear. I am cold and I am hungry. COME GET ME!"* We jumped in the jeep and headed towards the mountain. He was waiting humbly outside a store several miles from the campground. This was before the days of cell phones and he had walked all this way to find a phone! Only he knew what went through his mind and heart during this experience. We laughed at Hank, in a loving way of course, but realized it was the guy we knew so well and wouldn't change a thing about him - and the rest of his story? He did win that beautiful girl back. Hank, in his flip-flops and flashy car was like that young woman hiking around in her red boots. He just wanted to be loved for who he was. Square pegs… round holes… A lifetime can pass before a person realizes that they just might never fit in that round hole. Some people never come to that realization and waste their entire life away.

It seems I had forever been attempting to reshape myself to fit into round holes that I just never would fit into. Even when the little girl with glasses traded them in for contacts, I was still that "square peg." I recall the young college woman who had finally come into her own, but still sat in a booth at the student center a distance away from the "sorority sisters." The more I watched them, the more I celebrated my uniqueness. Over time though, ironically, I also found my own "sorority" of sorts with those who felt the same way I did. It is just human nature to gravitate to the comfortable, the familiar. So in the end, this "square peg" came home from college none the wiser, still trying to be accepted but not totally exhibiting acceptance in return. Do we ever stop? Do we ever step outside of ourselves even for a moment? To quote a line from my favorite movie Sabrina, *"I had to escape - and I did, to 'Paris.' I wrote in my stupid journal and I cut my stupid hair and I came back stupider than ever."* All these years later, it seems I still fall prey to those around me trying to push this square peg into that round hole. Tonight, I find comfort in my own skin. Perhaps it's simply age, but I think it is mostly due to the long journey of healing and the road towards restoration that I have been walking deep in my heart.. I have never been more pleased to be a "square peg." If you are not one, please walk a mile in my boots before you pass judgment.

Prejudice never seems to fully disappear no matter how old a person becomes. It is obvious by how many churches and political platforms we have. Several years ago, a group of women reminded me of those prejudices that never die. They were beautiful, articulate and educated. All but one was blond-haired and blue-eyed... perfect all-American specimens of womanhood. They were all school teachers, in fact. One had even been chosen as "teacher of the year!" The irony of their position in life is that they gathered in the parking lot of a movie theatre like some of their own school children - bullies there to vindicate their friend who was not happy that I had something in life that she did not - a certain man in my life. *They surrounded us and our vehicle like a gang on a playground. I must admit, I was taken aback and quite shocked. The insults that came afterwards spoke of my "southern" accent, my crossed eye, my "old lady" physique, my short hair and my broken past. This "square peg" did not fit into their round hole!* I have never been more proud to be a simple cross-eyed southern girl. As I sat there, holding my tongue with an air of grace and strength, I thought about all those cruel words they had spoken to me. My southern accent spoke words of love in a way that I would not dream of changing. I could even lift my voice with that accent and pray for the very ones who made fun of me. My not so straight big brown eyes had learned how to love others to where I could look into their loving eyes and see a reflection of my own loving heart. Those same eyes had found a way to look past a person's actions to their heart "crossed eye" and all. My wounded heart had found a way over the years to become a balm of healing for other hearts in pain. My weakness was made perfect in divine strength. A mile in my boots had taken me to places I never dreamed. What a road I had traveled on my journey from that brown-eyed girl with the curly locks - strutting around in white go go boots. The road had led the innocent baby girl straight to womanhood walking a path she didn't expect to be on, sometimes shaking in her grown up girl boots, but stronger than she knew and wiser than she would've been had she not walked those extra miles.

CHAPTER 22

IN THE SHADOWS

"It wasn't my ex-husband and all the abuse I had endured at his hands that was holding me back, it was ME and my refusal to forgive. I cried and wept into the night - face down on the floor, I squalled like a baby."

Dating in mid-life can be a scary thing. There is absolutely NOTHING simple about it. No matter how much we try to deny it, all of us who have been married and divorced, or at the very least been in a committed relationship, have carried more baggage than the cargo compartment of a 747. There is inevitably "stuff" of some sort. Some of that baggage is quite heavy on those extra miles on the detours of life after a break up.. Not only is the baggage heavy to carry, sometimes the road gets a bit winding and you find yourself in places you never expected and situations you would not have planned for yourself. I had traveled so many "out of the way" miles through relationships that my insecure heart had led me into. Disintegration of my first marriage and the scars that had caused, had led me on so many detours. There were days when I wondered how it might've been to be one of those girls like I went to high school and college with. They met their spouse early on, married, had children and lived the typical life that every young girl dreams about. The truth is, I have spoken to many of those girls from days gone by and that dream hasn't been picture perfect. It requires the work of both on a continuous basis to survive and thrive. Well, regardless of what could've been or should've been, my journey had been what it was. A major lesson for me through the many miles of my journey, is that regrets are such a waste of time. I had chosen rather, to find purpose in each step along the way.

Well, one of those "out of the way" places that I have personally experienced is a place I call "the shadows." Perhaps you know what I mean. The previous companion is bigger than life - positively or negatively, depending on who ended the marriage or relationship. It seems that even though you've received the curtain call to receive credit for all you've done and who you are, you are upstaged by the leading actress or actor and are forever waiting in the shadows or the wings for "your" moment behind the leading lady or man. Either there are comparisons as to all they did right or concerns that you, too, might do some of those wrong things they did - so either you are competing against an illusion or fighting a fear, but either way, it seems like life is lived in the shadows. I've experienced times where I put a foot forward to step up on that "stage" only to be pushed back into my place of waiting. I suppose the men in my life have felt exactly the same way. Sometimes it is not the former companion, but friends or activities that became a security blanket after divorce that one is too afraid to let go of to embrace relationship again. We all have baggage and handle our pasts differently. I read not too long ago something that said *"Everyone has baggage. Be grateful for the one who is willing to stay around to help you unpack."* Yes, starting over can be daunting and it takes great love and patience of both partners to work through the process.

As I look back on my "shadow" experiences, I can't help but smile and shake my head! I've sat at home while my spouse left me and my pre-schooler at ten p.m. so he could drive an hour and a half round trip to pick up something for his children to have for lunch because their mother would not go back out to the store. I've sat in the floor at one a.m. with my phone glued to my ear, patiently listening to my "boyfriend" talk about a previous relationship that he still could not understand. I've read letters from an ex-wife that expressed her desire to have "my" husband back in her life. My oh my! We all come into new relationships with some fractured pieces do we not? Also, divorce by its very nature, sometimes leaves one with a damaged self-image. It is just part of the casualty of divorce. That is why I am more compelled than ever to step up on my soapbox to share encouragement to others who have been beaten down, belittled and had their self-esteem whittled away. There is a place of love, respect and honor for you. Believe in yourself and your worth, and know that with the right person, at the right time, you will be ushered "on stage." Through my experiences, I realize that my Maker is the director of this "play." He will shine His spotlight on me at just the right moment. God knew what He was doing when he mandated the "death do us part" clause. Anything less requires a special measure of grace and mercy for all involved. Anyone who finds themselves in a new relationship after divorce learns this lesson one way or the other. It is inevitable. There will be comparisons. There will be times that you feel as if you are second place. The key is not to allow yourself become second place! If you do, you will find nothing but anger at those in your life, at those in your companion's life and at yourself. "Second place" is more of an illusion than a reality, and a reflection of how you are feeling about "you," more so than how your companion feels about you. Yes, set boundaries to protect how you feel, but at the same time, be realistic and objective. There was "life" before you just as there was "life" before him or her. Do not punish your present companion for past hurts that have nothing to do with them. They are NOT your ex! Also, believe in your own worth. People, even good people will treat you how you allow them to treat you. Sometimes it is callousness and sometimes it is just habit or lack of understanding as to how a situation is affecting you. Through it all, allow divine love to cover. It truly does cover all in a way that we cannot do alone. IT IS HARD SOMETIMES BUT WORTH EVERY EFFORT TO KNOW DIVINE LOVE! Don't carry unresolved hurt, anger or bitterness from your past relationship into a present one. If it is still there, then the hard truth is you are not ready for a new relationship. I learned that I could not hold on to my anger or nurse my hurt or even retaliate with words against people who had done me wrong. Un-forgiveness, harbored anger and resentment do not hurt the perpetrator of your hurt nearly as much as they hurt you! I walked my first long road towards forgiveness over twenty years ago. The hurt and pain and total devastation I felt after leaving my son's father in our marriage was paralyzing. I was angry at him and angry at myself. I simply was frozen and could not find a way to pick up the pieces and move forward in my life. One evening, I felt as if an elephant had sat on my chest. The weight of it all was just unbearable. I lay face down in the floor and began to weep. That supernatural whisper began to speak to my heart. *It wasn't my ex-husband and all the abuse I had endured at his hands that was holding me back, it was ME and my refusal to forgive. I cried and wept into the night - face down on the floor, I squalled like a baby.* Finally the release came, and with that release, un-forgiveness gave way to love - not as much for him as for myself. I had to forgive myself. This was a life lesson that I have carried with me all these years - sometimes successful and other times a struggle. It is one that holds true whether you find yourself being cast aside from a relationship or "in the shadows" of a relationship - be it on the job, in the church or community, neighborhood or in a family. Sometimes others just demand attention and do anything to have the preeminence. At times, people will walk on you and undermine you to get what they want. Don't allow others insecurities rob your self-esteem and self-worth. If you expect others to treat you with respect, it must begin with "you" treating yourself with respect.

When I was a freshman in college, we were inducted to college life with the dare of conquering the dreaded "curfew." Our campus was a Christian campus with rather strict rules. The doors to the dorms locked promptly at eleven p.m. each week night. It became our mission to find a way around that curfew at risky costs. One night, a group of girls kept watch for the campus police as they routinely patrolled the parking lots below our windows. As soon as the last flash light beam faded from the dorm wall and the coast was clear, a handful of us slipped out the side fire escape window into the parking lot that belonged to the boys' dorm. Unknowingly to us, the boys had caught wind of our escapade and were ready and waiting with an arsenal of water balloons. The boys were never held to the same curfew standard as the girls, so they stood boldly at their posts of defense. We, however, were taking refuge and cover under parked cars, bushes and anything that would provide minimal protection. Soon, however, the "commanders" caught wind of the ambush and decided to join the fight. The campus police brought their cars and parked them towards our dorm, with headlights shining so that we could not retreat and then began canvassing the parking lot. We scrambled like ants out of a disrupted mound. The boys took mercy on their prisoners and began diverting our enemy and then providing hideouts. Before I knew what had happened, I ended up being toted like a sack of potatoes under the arm of one of the boys and I was shoved in the side door of the boy's dorm - literally from the frying pan to the fire if I were caught! Some of the other girls were shoved into cars. We were all eventually reunited in one car and carried to an off-campus apartment. All of us that is, but one. My friend Rhoda was nowhere to be found. We all piled in the middle of the floor of this tiny apartment like the barracks of Stalag 13. Sleep evaded us as we wondered and worried about Rhoda. Had our friend been captured? Returned to the dorm? A knock came at the door. We were afraid to breathe. It was our friend. She had found refuge in a field of shrubbery and bushes at the edge of the parking lot. She lay in the grass for over an hour before someone helped her escape. In the midst of all the "girl chatter," exhilaration gave way to exhaustion and we finally drifted off to sleep. With the light of day and the six a.m. dorm door opening, all was right again and we were able to return "home."

All these years later, I still smile at this rather idiotic thing we did "back in the day." I look back on my life. I can't totally blame others. At times, I have lived in the shadows due to my own carelessness or insecurities. Those shadows are scary things. Thank God for love that canvassed the "bushes" and found me when I was hiding and afraid. At other times, I have lived in the shadows of life, experience and opportunity, simply waiting. We truly do spend much of life waiting don't we? What we must realize is that waiting serves a great purpose in life. We are studying, we are learning, we are being set aside for a more perfect performance than the opening act. It has been said that it is not as much about how many breaths you take, as it is in how many moments that take your breath away. Sometimes we can accomplish more with one significant action or word than a lifetime of chatter or busyness. Tonight, I find myself in one of those "waiting in the wings" or "in the shadows" moments. I am reminded of the Christmas play I was in as a girl. I was given the role of the angel announcing the birth of the Christ child. I stood "in the wings" waiting for my turn to step onto the stage. *"Don't be afraid. I bring you good news that will bring great joy to all people..."* The words were few but profound. Somehow, I feel very close to that little "angel" announcing the birth of the Savior. It seems I have been waiting "in the wings" or the shadows my whole life to share a message of love that burns deeply within my heart. Perhaps I will only have this one moment to step out of the shadows. If I do, the message is the same. There is good news. We are not lost or alone in this world. We don't have to be afraid.

CHAPTER 23

TUG OF WAR

"One evening, I stood in my bedroom - utterly exhausted. On one side, I felt gentle loving hands reaching for me and on the other a set of cruel spiteful hands pulling at me... It truly was a battle for my serenity and even my very life, I sensed."

Today was one of those rare days. I woke early - before the sun came up actually. My body was completely free of pain and my mind was absent from the fog that covers it on occasion. My heart seemed light and my soul free. As a member of the human race, these perks are not always the case. Sometimes, the wear and tear of life pulls us in so many directions that we feel like the instrument of a rugged game of tug of war. At times, it is my body desiring to rest but being pulled by the weight of responsibility that won't allow it. Sometimes, it is my heart longing to be all things to all those who love me yet feeling pulled apart - satisfying the need of no one, it seems. It is a juggling act to be a companion, a mother, a daughter, a friend, an employee - everyone vying for your attention and losing sight of what your own heart feels, wants and needs. As of late, I have learned so much more about balance in this game. It is kind of like a game of tug of war. When I keep equal weight and strength in perfect balance on each side, I am not drug into the "mud." It is only when I allow myself to be pulled in certain directions that I feel that tug into the abyss. I've learned that if I don't stand up for what my heart and soul feels is right, I'll be pulled apart like a rag doll. Woman was created to be the heart of relationships, home and family, and when we ignore that heart, everyone and everything is pulled apart. This is why it is so important to protect that precious heart. This is a lesson I waited much too long to learn.

When I was a young girl, one of my most favorite places to visit was a vacation spot called Smith Lake in north Alabama. My great Uncle Ed owned a big lake house there. It was like a Bed and Breakfast Inn or mountain chalet with its many bedrooms looking out over the lake, the big screened in porch and the rustic kitchen. In that kitchen, Mom and Maw Maw Weeks would make the best sandwiches, soups, hamburgers, eggs, pancakes or whatever else their creative palates would come up with. We would swim at the shallow banks of the lake or fish at its deeper edge. Upon a late afternoon arrival one year, we gathered up the fishing gear and headed out to the lake to see what was biting. Mostly it was the mosquitoes. I am normally not a very patient person, but when it comes to working on a project or participating in something like fishing, I will not quit until I achieve some measure of success or completion. On this day, the fish seemed to be in hibernation. After awhile, Dad grew weary as did my little brother. My mom and I, on the other hand, were there for the duration. After what seemed like hours, Mom's rod began to bend. She would pull and it would pull back. She would pull harder and it would bend with even more resistance. This one was a big one. Mother was becoming exhausted so I ran to get Dad. It was around dusk and the lake was surrounded in shadows. When Dad and I returned, Mom was still struggling with her big catch. Dad came over to help bring in this whopper of a fish. Upon closer examination, he said *"I've got to cut the line."* How dare he let that fish go after she had struggled so long and so hard! What she and I were not aware of is that her "fish" was actually a bush at the edge of the lake. She had been playing tug of war with a bush! My dad patiently pulled back the line and untwisted it enough to cut her free. I can certainly relate to times in my life when I, too, have been playing tug of war for success, for health, for relationship and a million other things, only to find that I've been pulled back and forth by a worthless "bush!" Perhaps it was my own fault - "fishing" at dusk when I could not clearly see what I was up against. Nothing is more painful than to work so long and so hard only to have to "cut the line," yet sometimes, "cutting the line" is required if we are to be truly free.

During those years when I was at my worst physically and the doctors had not determined the cause or the cure, I genuinely felt tug of war going on - in my body, mind, spirit and emotions. We knew about the Fibromyalgia, which in itself was a constant struggle, but there was something more that was totally debilitating me. I had become a prisoner in my own home, not able to even get out of bed for an hour, and really preferring to try and sleep anyway because the pain in the right side of my head and down the right side of my body was excruciating. Each day seemed like a fight to live and survive. I hated to even look at myself in the mirror. It was like staring at a skeleton covered by skin. My eyes were sunken deep in their sockets with dark circles surrounding them, and I had become so thin and pale. Every inch of my body hurt. It even hurt to blow dry my hair. ***One evening, I stood in my bedroom - utterly exhausted. On one side, I felt gentle loving hands reaching for me and on the other a set of cruel spiteful hands pulling at me.*** You've seen the cartoons where there is an "angel" on one shoulder and a "devil" on the other whispering in each ear. It was much more than that on this particular night. ***It truly was a battle for my serenity and even my very life, I sensed.*** *"Why in the world do you love God? He hasn't healed you, you can't work, your bills are piling up, you opened your heart up to love again and he left you to marry someone else, and you can't take care of your son. Why not just give up and denounce your faith?"* The tug was strong and the argument seemed valid in a mind that was stricken with pain and turmoil. On the other side, however,

I felt another set of strong hands ever so carefully loosening the line to untwist it. *"I need to cut the rope. Are you ready to let it all go?"* I had pulled at this weight, this anger, this grief, this fear and disappointment for so long. Finally, the words that I had been searching for found their way from my heart. *"I don't believe and trust in God because of what He can do for me. I center my life in Him because I love Him. He has already provided ALL for me. What more could I ask?"* I understood all too well that the lack in my life was not the Divine's fault. He didn't make me sick, He didn't put me in debt and He didn't choose the man that I had loved that walked away. He didn't burden me with stress or cripple me with worry. The illness was just part of life. The debt was due to the choice I had made in a companion who was not prepared to walk in financial freedom and be the provider and partner in life that a woman needs and deserves. The stress and worry were because I had allowed myself to give in to hurt and pain and caused my body to suffer even more. I couldn't blame God for any of it. The tugging at my soul and heart ceased. Thinking of that night those years ago causes my heart to sing once more even though life continues to pull at me and my emotions get hung up on things that simply do not matter. From that night until now, through all my struggles and all of life's tug of war, I have never forgotten "Who" holds my lifeline. I am reminded often that we are not alone on the journey. Yes, sometimes my stubbornness and strong will tug at the lifeline - all while the Universe tries to free me from the pull again. God is there gently untangling the line, longing to cut me free from those things that weigh me down.

CHAPTER 24

THREE DOLLAR BOTTLE OF LIFE

"Months went by, the migraines intensified, the pain was unbearable until at times, I literally wanted to cut open the side of my head for a small amount of relief. I felt as if I were losing my mind. My body became weaker and my right eye completely crossed from the pain."

Those years ago as my illness became so debilitating, I found it imperative to make some lifestyle changes. One, was that I veered away from drinking soft drinks, both for the sugar content as well as the caffeine. Both were like poison to my system and would cause devastating Fibromyalgia flare ups. I began drinking bottled water and before long, my son was hooked on the stuff too. It's amazing what a simple bottle of water can do. We can live without food for some time, but only a few days without water. What a precious commodity this clear liquid is. It is literally like drinking from the fountain of life.

Not too long ago, my brother, sister-in-law and nephew were on a trip. After their departure, something went haywire with the electrical system in their SUV. The windows would not roll up or down. The power locks were stuck and the air conditioning quit working. My father met them to trade cars with them and brought theirs back to have it serviced. He asked me to do some research on the internet to see if anyone else had experienced similar problems with this particular model of car. I did find a similar case, and it turned out to be a simple wire in the electrical system in the door panel of the car. All of that difficulty was resolved by something so simple. Sometimes the most difficult of life's problems or complexity of circumstance can be resolved with the simplest of solutions. It is just a matter of knowing where to look, being willing to hang on and being determined to never give up.

During those first couple of years when my health began to fail me, I was tested for everything under the sun. I had x-rays, MRI's, spinal taps, nerve conduction studies, blood work and more blood work. I was tested for Lupus, Multiple Sclerosis, brain tumors, cancer - you name it I was tested for it. About six months after the symptoms began, my cousin Cathy called and asked me to accompany her to a women's conference. She was asked to speak and asked if I would come and sing and share my story. Physically I was not up to par, but emotionally needed to make this leap of faith. After the meeting, a woman came up to me and said *"I know exactly what is wrong with you."* I had not really shared my physical symptoms, only that I had been battling a condition for a few months. She asked me to describe my symptoms to her. In response, she told me she had been experiencing the same thing that literally was draining the life out of her. It turned out that she had a severe B-12 deficiency. She said that she began to immediately improve once she started on monthly shots. I was so encouraged to hear that perhaps something simple could be the source of my issues as well. Besides, it had to be a divine act for this woman to discern what I was going through without me sharing it at all. I could not wait to return to my neurologist to speak with him about this possibility. Much to my shock and disbelief, he totally dismissed the idea. Even though she and I had the exact same symptoms he was unwilling to order a blood test to at least rule this out. He was certain that he had it all figured out. I had been deficient of iron as a girl and it only stood to reason to me that I could have yet another deficiency. But, he was the expert, I wasn't.

Months went by, the migraines intensified, the pain was unbearable until at times, I literally wanted to cut open the side of my head for a small amount of relief. I felt as if I were losing my mind.

My body became weaker and my right eye completely crossed from the pain. From February until December, I pleaded with my doctor to order up the blood test. Finally, he resigned himself to the fact that doctors do not know everything and ordered a special test. The next day I received his phone call. The lady from the conference had been right all along. The test showed that I had an antibody in my system that rejects B-12 and I was severely deficient of this life-giving vitamin. Its lack in my system was totally destroying my neurological system. The damaged nerves could've repaired themselves if it had been within six months, but the time had long since come and gone thanks to a stubborn, self-absorbed doctor. I was instructed to begin shots immediately. At first it required three shots a week, then two, one and finally a couple of shots a month for the rest of my life. I was so angry and hurt. All I had needed all of that time was a three dollar bottle of liquid B-12. Three dollars a month had been standing between me and life! Because of the delay, I would suffer neurological pain to some degree the rest of my life.

How easy it is to condemn my doctor for refusing to explore this simple solution. Ironically, I had been doing the same thing with my life - not physically, but mentally, emotionally and spiritually. Issues through my life had been draining the very life out of me and bringing more pain than I could imagine and all along there was a supernatural answer. I was too wise, too stubborn and too afraid to accept my Creator's bottle of life, His "balm of healing." Sometimes we do things for so long, say things so often and behave in such a manner that we not only convince others, but convince ourselves. We think we are doing what is right. On the outside it certainly seems so, but internally, our motives and thoughts are all out of sorts. We are depleting ourselves of the life-giving flow of our Maker and of the universe by trying to handle things ourselves. Even "right" things done in the wrong way or for the wrong reason can debilitate us and hinder the healing flow. If we cover up the symptoms long enough or ignore them continually, one day we will wake up to find something of value has died in us or at the very least has suffered irreparable damage. I had spent years moving forward, continuing to do what I thought was right - basically staying as busy as possible to avoid the hurt and pain inside. After awhile, I became numb to it all. This reminds me of a story of a young boy that I read about some time ago. He had a rare disease in his body that prevented him from feeling any pain. Now that may sound like a blessing in disguise, but pain is a necessary indicator for us. His father told of a day when the child's mother had put cookies in the oven to bake. The little boy wanted a cookie, so he simply opened the oven, pulled out the hot pan to get a cookie. Because he could not feel the pain, he received severe burns. I think I had done the same thing with my mind, emotions and heart. I had become so numb, that I was burned worse through each experience and wasn't even aware for so long. The answer had been pulling at me always, but I had pulled back and refused to let go or give in. What was so simple, had become so complicated. My physical solution through the vitamin deficiency issues had given me a great life lesson. Like my B-12 injections that are there in my drawer to access weekly to restore my body, so are the answers to the hurts of my heart and soul. However, if I forget or refuse to administer them, what good are they? Such it is with the divine healing power of God. I can hurt and cry, grieve and despair or I can find relief and hope by simply turning to Him and allowing Him to pour the oil of His love and goodness into my hurting soul. It is in Him that I continue to find both relief and resolve just as I did those years ago - relief in that He alleviates my pain, but also resolve. I accept the fact that I have scars; scars that will be visible for the rest of my life. To me though, those scars are beautiful. They are a part of who I am and a gentle reminder of a mended heart and life.

CHAPTER 25

WINDOW OF THE SOUL

"I had spent my whole life overcoming this inferior feeling I had due to my vision disability, hiding it with contacts so I could feel beautiful and then he tells me it is a roadblock!"

It is one of those days when I realize my age in a multitude of ways. Getting older is a mixed bag of goods, for sure! Unfortunately it is not one of those pain free days. Today, little aches and pains accompanied me upon waking and my eye sight is causing one of those nasty migraines. These are just my regular "thorns in the flesh" reminding me that I am "not all that" without human understanding and acceptance and divine love. It is on days like today that I must reach out for the soothing touch of others, or the calming voice of my Maker. I don't want to ever forget again that all I need is right in front of me. I don't have to deal with difficult days alone - ever! Love is all around me. It is my choice whether to receive or reject it each day.

Years ago, after Husband Number Two, "love" crept up on me rather unexpectedly and found its way into my heart before I had the chance to resist. Love is like that. It appears in the most unlikely of places and people. A lady from my church was working for a man that she felt I *"just had to meet"* and he *"just had to meet me."* Ms. Dot just "knew" we were perfect for each other. Ms. Dot was a lady who knew what she wanted and was relentless until she achieved whatever it was that she had in her mind to do. She was all of five feet tall and ninety pounds soaking wet, but she was a powerhouse! She was a bit outspoken and extremely candid, and sometimes I truly wished I could be just a bit more like her! This man and

I reluctantly agreed to speak to each other by phone and then see from there if we might want to meet. We were both very upfront about our intentions. I did not want to date again and neither did he. He had been through a long hurtful relationship and I had come out of marriage number two trying again to build my life. I simply DID NOT want a man! So this green-eyed man, with the salt and pepper hair, showed up one Sunday to hear me sing, took me to lunch and we soon realized that time together was exactly what we wanted. We became friends and in time, the inevitable happened and the line was eventually crossed between friendship and romance. Here we both were again - two wounded hearts trying to find healing in each other. I had still not realized that it just wasn't possible. Two wounded hearts do not make the best combination. In matters of love, two halves do not make a whole. How ironic it seems in hindsight. The very first day we met, he made a statement that I had heard and adopted as my "mantra" months before. *"Two people should not come together to compliment or complete each other. They both should be complete in themselves and complement each other as a result."* It seemed that this was a lesson in progress for both of us.

It was during this dating relationship that I began to experience the severe health problems due to the B-12 deficiency. The migraines had become severe at that time, and as a result, my right eye had begun crossing. One day he and I were sharing a tender quiet moment when out of the blue he felt the need to be totally honest with me. While I respected his honesty, sometimes, some things are better left unsaid. He looked at me and said *"I feel so close to you and truly want to know you more but sometimes when I look at you in the eyes, I am hindered. I feel that the eyes are the window of the soul and I just can't look as deep as I need to because of the condition with your eye."* I was devastated! ***I had spent my whole life overcoming this inferior feeling I had due to my vision disability, hiding it with contacts so I could*** *feel beautiful and then he tells me it is a roadblock!* Things progressed with us for awhile, but I never forgot that statement. Over the course of our time seeing each other, he must've told me I was beautiful, sophisticated and amazing a million times or more, but for the million plus positives, that one negative stayed with me. Needless to say, this man was not with me as my health issues progressed. If a "weak eye" was too much for him, I can only imagine how debilitating sickness would've affected him, so I chose to keep my health concerns a secret from him. He was a very good and kind man, but I would not burden him with something that he obviously was not ready to deal with. The one positive from this transparent moment for both of us, is a lesson I've carried with me all these years. It is to your benefit to be upfront about expectations in a relationship, because the deeper you become involved, the greater the hurt if there is something that you simply cannot get past. It is better to face the truth than to try and convince yourself and the other person that you can "accept" something that you know deep in your gut that you can't.

One day I was talking to a close friend about my grandmother. I had grave concerns about her driving. She, also, had minimal vision in one eye and could barely see out of the other yet at almost 90 years old, she was still driving herself to church, to the store and to the bank. I was asking my friend to say extra prayers for her that day. He just laughed and said *"Well sweetie you can only see out of one eye too so I guess we need to say prayers for both of you."* This teasing I can lovingly take from him, a friend who not only tells me I am beautiful, but shows me by peering deep into my soul, my heart. It was only fitting that he was the one by my side when I had corrective eye surgery last year.

It is amazing what we adults allow to stand in our way. Life has a way of causing our hearts to become jaded. We lose that childlike simplicity that brings acceptance. We set stipulations and criteria for others but expect total acceptance in return. Early last year prior to my eye surgery, I was waiting inside a restaurant for some Chinese take-out. It is one of my favorite little spots to grab a quick meal for my family on a busy day. The owner of the restaurant has a little girl. She is about eight years old and one of the most precious little girls I've ever known. Watching her animated expression on that beautiful face of hers and listening to her speak perfect English as her parents speak Chinese, brings a smile to my face. I stand in awe of a little one that can master two languages - two complicated ones at that! Each time I come in, she makes her way over to me and asks me to play some sort of game with her while I am waiting on my food. That day I went in had been a very long day and I was extremely tired. Usually, when I was tired, my weak right eye crossed even more than it normally would. As we talked and played, she stopped and without reservation asked *"What happened to your eye?"* Well, I was not put off by it in the least. I simply told her the story of how I had damaged it as a little girl when younger than her and how it had weakened over the years of my life. She accepted my answer and we went right on playing our game. My eye was not a "show stopper" for this little girl. When my order was ready and I got up to leave, she made sure to give me a big bear hug before I left. Oh the love of a child - straight from Gods heart. Through that love I feel beautiful, inside and out.

Yes, it is true that the *"eyes are the window of the soul,"* but sometimes, I think it is the mouth that reveals what is deep inside - *"out of the abundance of the heart the mouth speaks."* This certainly proved to be true with my ex-boyfriend and also with my special little friend. What a sobering thought. In an effort to gauge our words, we should interpret words already spoken as to why they are said - both our words and the words spoken to us from others. They are like the bit in the mouth of a horse able to guide in ways that can be rewarding or extremely destructive. There is a wise proverb that states that there is literally *"life and death in the power of the tongue."* Why, I can't really say, but it seems that I have allowed "words" direct my course my entire life. Unfortunately in times past, it was more the words of others than my own. Perhaps this is the very reason that I have chosen "words" as a venue to help, heal and encourage. Perhaps, I need them like that bit in the horse's mouth to direct me along the way. It is no doubt that I never feel more at home than when I am able to release the words stirring around in my head and heart. My hands fly like lightening across this keyboard emitting words like static electricity. Today, I find myself remembering words, words and yet more words… some recent and some from days gone by. Some of them pierce my soul like a knife. Others provide a soft place to land and warm my heart. As I read the words on the crisp white page in front of me, I began to get a glimpse of myself once again. So I write, endlessly… I write, peering into the window of my soul a little more each day.

CHAPTER 26

THE LIGHT OF DAY

"On this particular night, one of those summer storms found its way to where we were. The wind was howling, the trees were bending like rubber bands and lightening darted the sky like fireworks. As I tried to sleep in the back of the trailer, I kept hearing a scratching outside. It sounded as if someone was trying to get in."

I have a visitor that creeps into my room each morning. His name is "Daylight" and no matter how softly or tenderly he tiptoes into the room, his presence is undeniable. He showed up again this morning on the most wonderful, crisp, cool fall day. I am amazed at how powerful, yet how tender his presence can be. He can travel at the speed of 186,282 miles per second with such incredible power and velocity, yet land gently on the eyes of a sleeping baby and never awaken it. I can beckon for his presence in the darkest of night, yet with all of that speed and power, he arrives methodically and consistently around the same moment each day. With his arrival, all that I had heard rustling in the shadows or failed to see in darkness the night before, changes. Everything is clearer in the light of day. I wonder. Why are we so afraid of the dark? Why do we spend so much time stumbling in the darkness instead of resting and waiting for daylight to appear? Has it ever failed to appear? No… it is that constant companion that shows up each day like a faithful friend no matter what.

Years ago, I used to travel - singing in various venues and living in a thirty-two and half foot travel trailer when on the road. This was the time of my life when I was faithfully devoted to my husband and his outreach, despite the turmoil that was our lives behind closed doors. The positive thing that kept me going for so long, was to actually see so many people make decisions to change their destructive path in life - teens in a high school gym or addicts in recovery, battered women at shelters or families at conferences and church services. My heart was so broken each time that I encountered people. Each one of them were much more like me than they knew - people with broken lives, struggles, fears, secrets and a million things in between. Each of them, each of us, were just on a daily quest for peace, worth, acceptance and unconditional love. All of humanity is much more kindred in nature than we fully admit or realize.

One night in our travels, we were parked in a less than desired part of town. *On this particular night, one of those summer storms found its way to where we were. The wind was howling, the trees were bending like rubber bands and lightening darted the sky like fireworks. As I tried to sleep in the back of the trailer, I kept hearing a scratching outside. It sounded as if someone was trying to get in.* I made my way to the front of the trailer and peered outside. Nothing was there, it seemed. Each time I would give in to sleep, the tapping outside would begin. Was someone trying to pry open a window? Shimmy open the door? It proved to be a long, exhausting night. With the light of day, I found the courage to step outside to assess the previous night's situation. I found my "intruder." It was the limb of a tree that had been scraping up against the trailer as the wind bent it back and forth. Such it is in life. In time, when the light of understanding, knowledge, wisdom, love and patience is shed on our fears, our anxieties, our insecurities and our doubts, things are not nearly as daunting or intimidating as they seemed in the dark.

It is amazing what a new day can bring. The secret is to start each day new and fresh like it was intended to be. Sometimes though, we are like the character "Pig Pen," Charlie Brown's friend from the Peanuts gang. We have this "cloud" that follows us everywhere we go. Shadows from yesterday cloud the light of a new day. New relationships are smothered from the shadow of old ones. Job opportunities are lost in the clouds of past failures. I am eternally optimistic, but have moments like everyone, struggling to shake the dust from yesterday off my feet so I can walk freely through today. It's like starting out on a trip with the parking brake partially on. You may move slowly but will burn up quickly.

The summer between my junior and senior year of college, I made a decision to stay in town and keep working at my work-study job with the school. I missed going home for summer vacation, but felt it was a good trade-off since I loved my job and didn't want to risk losing it. So, I endured the loneliness by working full-time and allowing summer students keep me company. My boyfriend called and wrote all summer, and finally, he and all my friends were on their way back! I had made it. One morning I went into work only to hear the most disturbing news. The college was experiencing some financial setbacks and had to cutback. They were deleting our entire department and we were losing our jobs. I had endured the whole summer for this job only to hear I was losing it! Later that evening, my boyfriend called and said he had made it back and wanted to come over to my apartment to see me. At least this was some solace. I had missed him terribly! By the end of the evening, however, I was ready to crawl in a hole and die somewhere. After the "*let's be friends*" speech, I felt as if I was surround by a dark cloud. We had written and called all summer only for him to decide he wanted to date others. As is with the life of a college student, however, the light of day the next morning brought a whole new perspective.

That young woman was so resilient. As I reflect on all that I have experienced in life and have come through since those college days long ago, I realize I have become even more resilient through the years. Many times people ask how I can smile given all that life has thrown my way or that I have stumbled into. I don't know if I have an answer to that. I suppose I realize that gratitude is a better alternative. What other option is there? When we survive difficult moments, what a waste to allow those past moments steal what we have today. Our past is simply a testing ground providing lessons for today and tools for our future. Now that I am learning to take reflective long looks inside that "window of my soul," I am finding the strength and courage to dispel the shadows of yesterday. As I do, I realize even more that the young woman from long ago is still rather resilient. I recall yesterday morning when my heart was heavy over a deep hurt and tears were flowing like a river. Somewhere during the day, the light of love from the One who pursues me each day illuminated my dark spirit and the tender care and affection of those close to me brought encouragement. Today, life is fresh and hope springs eternal. I think I am like that old toy the "Weeble Wobble." Do you remember? *"Lovable Weebles help your kids learn about their world and what families do...Weebles wobble but they don't fall down..."* No matter how many times you try to knock them over they bounce right back up! Even after all these years, I find myself waking as I did this morning to the light of day realizing that no matter what yesterday presented to me or what last night dumped on me, I still have today and no one can take that from me. No one can darken it except for me. The truth is, I am the only one responsible for my life and destiny. Just as I chose to open my window blind to daylight this morning, I can choose to open my heart to the light of all that is mine for the taking...

CHAPTER 27

THIS TOO SHALL PASS

"When I arrived, I sat down almost afraid to breathe. I was already struggling enough in some of my other classes, and as much as I loved this class, I didn't want it to be among those. The professor took a deep breath and then he just smiled for a moment. It was as if I could sense the compassion of God Himself on my professor's face."

A few years ago, I attended Freshman Orientation at the university with my son. It was quite an experience and like a blast from the past. I perfectly understood why college life comes at an early age. My body would not be able to keep up at this point in life! I had totally forgotten what it was like to maneuver a large campus on a hot southern day. Over the course of the following few weeks, we scrambled to get everything worked out as far as Josh's financial aid, grants, loans, etc. I had submitted all of the paperwork except for one request. This particular application was for a parent loan on behalf of the student. Joshua had already been awarded a Pell Grant, Academic Scholarship and Stafford Loans, but I felt that I wanted to see if there was even more that I could do to help. Frankly, I was less than optimistic due to my financial situation at the time and the uphill climb I had faced rebuilding my credit over the last several years. I decided that it was worth the try. All they could do was say *"no."* A few days after I submitted the application, a letter made its way to me in the mail from the U.S. Department of Education. I braced myself for what I was certain would be the extent of the letter. But no! Much to my surprise the loan had been approved! It would be all that he would need for a computer, living and transportation expenses for the year. I was reminded of a passage in that sacred book I love - *"you have not because you ask not."* I've heard it said that if you never ask the answer will always be "no."

Sometimes it seems as if things in our lives are eternal, and sometimes I suppose they are. At times, health eludes us to never return. On other occasions, relationships disintegrate never to restore. Truly though, if we understood the divine timeline of our lives everything is eternal but nothing is permanent (outside of love of course). It is more like transition rather than finality. Our relationships morph from one phase to another, some people come and go for one reason or another, our health rises and falls also and life is perpetually changing. This is the way it is meant to be. Still, whether sick or well, single or coupled, rich or poor, some things remain even through transitions and changes. They may change in dynamics and purpose, but they remain. We still have those certain people in our lives who are by our side no matter who else might walk out of our lives, who are there for us no matter what. Their love is timeless. It may be family or close friends, but there is always someone who helps us realize that we are really never totally alone on our journey through all we face. That is a truth each of us needs to lay hold of - the fact that there is strength in community, in kinship and friendship. Unconditional love doesn't come and go it simply transitions from one phase to the next depending on what we need through each phase of our lives. The strength found through the care of others is something that we should treasure above all else. We were never meant to live isolated like an island in this world. The other constant in life is that we still have the same breath from our Maker circulating through our body reminding us that He is ever present even though life moves on in so many ways. As for everything else, personally, I am rather grateful for the transitions. Otherwise, some things would be unbearable. Imagine if life never changed!

Yes, we all move through many life transitions. Facing the real world in college, Josh learned even more about transitions, though he had experienced more than his share in life at such a young age. As he dove further into his college career, he faced the normal difficult moments that we all have during our school experiences. I know I faced a time during school that was extremely difficult for me. I had changed my major more than once, was behind on my requirements, had struggled with balance and was overwhelmed emotionally and physically. Illness continued to rear its ugly head and I was tired, so very tired. I suppose I could spend the rest of my life trying to understand "why" so much had piled in on me and why I could not overcome the struggles, but sometimes there are just no answers. Like Thomas Edison, all we can really do is learn all the ways that "don't work" in order to find the way that "does work" so that the "light" will eventually come on. For some it is slower than others. I have longed since learned that my growth has been at "oak" speed rather than "pine" speed. I have been criticized more than once for that. However, there is no doubt who will survive the storms and winds though! During this time of difficulty at college, I had a professor who was quite tuned in to his students. I suppose it was because he was a psychology professor. He could spot turmoil a mile away. One day after class, he stopped me and asked if I would come by his office. I was worried that maybe I had made a bad grade or was not doing as well as I thought. I had been making decent grades in his class, so I could not imagine what the issue was. *When I arrived, I sat down almost afraid to breathe. I was already struggling enough in some of my other classes, and as much as I loved this class, I didn't want it to be among those. The professor took a deep breath and then he just smiled for a moment. It was as if I could sense the compassion of God Himself on my professor's face.* *"I've sensed that you are going through some personal struggles Starla. I really don't even have to know or for that matter need to know what they are. All that I want to share with you is the truth of one little passage that says 'this too shall pass.' I know it may not seem like it now, but it will. Nothing is permanent and if you can grasp that, you will make it."* I don't really remember what, if much more that was said that day. Nothing more was truly needed. What I do remember is walking back across campus, fighting back tears and feeling as if a load of bricks had just been lifted off my shoulders. Life truly was bearable no matter what.

It is amazing how something seemingly so insignificant can make such an impact. I didn't learn this professor's lesson totally during my college experience sadly, but if I gained nothing more than that one moment, it was worth it all. I recall hearing those words in the recesses of my mind on days when I was neck deep in abuse and abandonment years later. Some of those days seemed eternal and I often would close my eyes hoping that I would wake up somewhere else. Though I am ashamed to admit it, sometimes, I closed my eyes hoping I would not wake up at all. Somehow I found solace in those words that still resounded in my ear from long ago *"this too shall pass."* One day, the pain and hurt would be over. My fair haired "angel" all those years ago had reminded me of that as well. I began speaking those words to my heart once again over the last few years when I was smothering in health and financial issues - burdens that were dumped on me after being left abandoned and alone to pick up the pieces from a third marriage. This marriage had developed on the heels of a second one that never should have been. What a journey my lonely, insecure heart had continued to take me on. This man was well aware of my sickness before the "I do's" and stated it didn't matter if I debilitated to the point that I was never able to work again or ended up in a wheelchair or worse. He loved me and wanted to take care of me and be with me forever. A "forever" that lasted a year, when he looked me in the eyes before walking out the door and said *"You are the kind of woman men would die to be married to, but I just don't want to be married."* I wish I could say I felt I had made a mistake with yet another marriage, but honestly I can't. I had been single a number of years, had prayed for guidance; we had counseled with our pastor who also felt a sense of peace and assurance that this marriage was a good thing. The marriage ceremony was a reverent moment. As we knelt at the prayer bench for the pastor to pray a blessing over us, we both cried like babies. Given that, all that I can say today to anyone who asks is that in life there are no guarantees. All we can do is follow our hearts and make the best decisions we can based on where we are. Mainly though, we must remain accountable to our higher power, to each other and to ourselves and work daily to stay in the Divine's plan and be all that we are able to be. It's pretty simple actually - stay true to God, stay true to your spouse, stay true to yourself. When we don't, life gets out of kilter and things fall apart no matter how much we pray they will not. I'm certain there were things I did wrong, we both did wrong. There is never just one person at fault in any situation. I can regret my failures, his failures, or I can forgive - him and myself and move on to take the lessons learned and strive to be the woman I was created to be. Marriage at its best is work, and it takes both being willing to work it through and not give up. One cannot hold a marriage together no matter how much they desire to. So yes, there was another divorce... one that was more devastating than ever, since I was at such a low point in every aspect. Like so many times before, despair once again passed. My health improved, life went on, and my spiritual "Father" continued to walk with me pouring in His precious balm of healing in my heart and soul. I survived! I look back and see just how far I have come. I am enjoying life and love with my family, my friends and I feel joy and true happiness that transcends all that has tried to hinder me. I've made more mistakes and felt more pain, but in it all, I understand. Yes, I truly see that the "thorns in the nest" have only served to give me wings to fly. Once again, I can honestly understand how eternal life is yet how temporal situations are… *"this too shall pass."* I remember times long ago when I had no food in my pantry or money in the bank because the addict spent it all on his latest fix. I recall periods of my life where I grieved over moments when I followed my fears instead of my faith. I look back to hours, days and weeks when I watched over my preemie baby and wondered if he would push out another breath. Somehow, I always remembered in the midst of it ALL *"this too shall pass,"* and somehow, it all did pass. Now, I look at Josh twenty-one years later heading out into adulthood. Yes, yes, yes *"this too shall pass."* This morning I received a text message from a friend that is a constant reminder of acceptance and all that truly matters. *"Good morning pretty girl."* Those words bring a smile to my face. So with caring words from a human heart, I am reminded that the things that are meant to remain will and those other things that try to steal our focus from the constants in our life, can be overcome. No matter what, all things are bearable and all things are possible simply because… *"this too shall pass."*

CHAPTER 28

WIN, WIN...

"I sat there with a dozen of our friends. We sang, we laughed, we cried and we shared stories. We watched and we waited. How strange. It did not seem like defeat. There was a celebration of her life in the air. I held her hand and felt her clasp mine tightly. Somehow, I felt that she knew we were there. A gasp came and one final breath and then, she was gone. Tonight, I miss my friend."

It is no secret that I love a good movie or that "chick flicks" will bring a tear to my eyes every time. Sometime ago, I watched the movie *"Confessions Of A Shopaholic."* Since it was a romance comedy, the only outcome possible was a good one. The story portrays a character who finally realizes the error of her ways after losing the man she loves. To bring order back to her life, she courageously decides to auction off every item that she purchased through her shopping addiction that had wreaked havoc in every area. She had allowed "things" to take the place of what she truly needed to fill the void in her heart and life. In a strange way, I could relate to this woman - not so much with "things" but with activities and people. I, too, had tried to fill the internal void through external means for way too many years.

The last item up for bid in the auction was an elegant emerald green scarf that the woman owned and had used as a prop for her writing byline of the magazine that she wrote for. The scarf had originally been paid for by the man she loved during their first encounter. It was symbolic of all that truly mattered to her - the man she loved and lost, and the job she had let slip through her fingers. The day of the auction, there was a bidder on the phone and one in person on the floor battling for this scarf. The scarf finally went to the highest bidder - a lovely young woman with blonde hair. It would be a flattering compliment to her eyes and hair. The bidder made her final offer and won this exquisite scarf. Later, the love of the shopaholic's life comes to her and to her surprise, he is holding the green scarf in his hand. He had been both the bidder on the phone and the bidder through the young blonde woman. Either way, he was going to win the one thing that meant most to the woman who held his heart and that symbolized their love. The purchase was a win, win.

I had a friend years ago that battled cancer. Mitzi was an outspoken, vivacious woman with an incredible zest for life. She was married, had two beautiful daughters, a handsome son, a tight circle of friends and a devoted husband. Time had changed things in multiple ways - the first being disintegration of her marriage. Who knows what drives people apart, but the result of this break-up brought out the worst in Mitzi. She was bitter, angry, spiteful and revengeful. In a word, she was hurting. Let me just say on a side note, I can relate to Mitzi. There have been times that I've heard words coming out of my mouth, or have seen actions that seemed to be that of a stranger whom I did not know at all. Mitzi portrayed hurt in much the same way. During all of her tirades, her ex-husband just stood there absorbing her verbal assault. Mitzi had battled cancer as well, so it was no wonder that she had so much pent up inside. After several years, she went into remission and grabbed life by the horns, once again. During the months that followed, however, the cancer showed up once more, with a vengeance and very little mercy. Once again, Mitzi began to change. This time though, the anger began to subside; the hurt gave way to resolve to a life better served in forgiveness and gratitude. She fought and fought hard, not against her ex-husband, but against death. She never gave up. In the process, the love of this couple was rekindled and this man of hers stood by her side taking the vows from years ago to heart "till death do us part." The cancer took over Mitzi's body until her bones were fragile and weak. One Sunday morning, she was sitting on the front pew at church with her arm in a sling. I came by and spoke to her and asked her what happened. She had rolled over in the night and her collar bone had broken because of the cancer. She just looked at me and laughed. *"One day girl you are going to come by me and have to pick my arm up off the floor!"*

On one occasion, Mitzi was sharing her story. I'll never forget the words she spoke that day. *"You see, either way it goes, I win. If I die, I win, if I live I win. Either way it is a win, win for me!"* I had always believed that I had a good attitude through my little "stuff" in life, but how "whiny" I had been by comparison. There really wasn't anything that I had lost to speak of. Why? Because all along "Someone" was in the background, loving me, and bidding for what meant the most to me without me even knowing it. Sometimes, we need to let go of all to get back everything.

There was one final day that I sat with Mitzi months after that Sunday encounter. This time, she lay in the hospital in a coma teeter-tottering between life and death, heaven and earth. *I sat there with a dozen of our friends. We sang, we laughed, we cried and we shared stories. We watched and we waited. How strange. It did not seem like defeat. There was a celebration of her life in the air. I held her hand and felt her clasp mine tightly. Somehow, I felt that she knew we were there. A gasp came and one final breath and then, she was gone. Tonight, I miss my friend.* In her dying, she showed us all how to live. Tonight, I grieve over every moment I've wasted and every lie I've believed. Tonight, I long for forgiveness from anyone I've let down or for the times my own lack has caused me to fall so short. Tonight, I feel sorrow for the unkind words I've spoken to those I love in anger. I am sad that I've allowed hurt to turn outward in the ways it has, at times. Tonight, I realize more than ever just how short and how fragile life is. I do not want to harbor ill will or continue to carry hurt towards anyone or them me. Again, life is too short. I do not want to spend so much time hung up on my issues or the issues of others that I let life pass me by. Tonight, I especially long for forgiveness for the hours I've taken my loving Divine "Father" for granted. Perhaps you don't believe in His existence. That is certainly your right. All I can tell you from my experience is that the "God moments" in my life are unquestionable. He's been there all along - bidding behind the scenes and through others just for me. In it all, I was hand delivered the one thing that I've longed for but lost in things of far less value. I reclaimed my self-esteem, I re-discovered my pure heart; I dug up the buried treasure of my soul. Tonight is a "win, win."

CHAPTER 29

I AM RICH

"I could not focus on either my abuse or his father's addiction any longer. My baby boy was my priority - not my well-being and not his father's recovery. It's peculiar how sickness, adversity and yes even death become the great 'equalizer' of all."

When I sit to read the news each day I am always amazed at just what a close-knit community we inhabitants of Earth are. I can learn of events an ocean away in a matter of moments. With modern communication, I can speak to someone clear across the world, be by their side in less than a day, or send a gift to them in a day's time that traveled clear across the ocean. Our world and its people are so diverse and everything, it seems, is relative. How can we be so close and yet so far apart as kindred citizens of this place we call home? We are so close, yet so detached even from the neighbors across the street and often from those sitting across the dinner table from us each night. One man's worries would be another's wish - if only he had that much opportunity to "worry" about. One man may be worrying how the shaky stock market is affecting his surplus investments in our present economy, while another is choosing between refilling a necessary prescription or purchasing a car tag that is about to expire. Yes, it is all relative. We are close, but yet so far apart in ways that do not have to be. We separate ourselves with the very things that could bring us together. What could be a bridge between two extremes, becomes a wall. Everything is relative.

Even worse is the person who sees no value in anything on either end of the spectrum. There was a story in our local paper sometime ago. It was about a young man who worked to acquire his engineering degree, obtained a good job with a reputable company and bought a nice home for himself. He wasn't rich but had worked very hard to make his young life comfortable. One evening, four men just a few years younger than him, barged into his home to see what they could take. He did not even have any money in the house. One of the four put a gun to his head and took what he could because he did not get what he wanted. Now, the young man's life is over and so are the lives of the four who stole that from him. Why do the "haves" and "have nots" build such walls? Where did we lose sight of the understanding that ALL life has value?

I was involved in a discussion once with a friend of mine. We were talking about the end of time if there were to be a global war or some other cataclysmic event. This had been an occasional topic of ours ever since watching the movie 2012. Everything of value now would change and other things would become as precious as gold. Money would be trash while weapons, food and provision would be treasures. Yes, everything is relative. Watching the news these days we are seeing that shift in the value of certain commodities over others. It is ironic how our priorities change during times of crisis or need. We suddenly realize what truly matters, what we truly value more than anything. The wealthiest person in the world would trade every last dime, if they had to choose between life, health or wealth. Yes, adversity causes us to realize what truly matters. During those first weeks and months after Joshua was born, I realized just how true this is. He was born after only twenty-six weeks of pregnancy. He weighed a whopping two pounds and one ounce, was thirteen and a quarter inches long and looked like a little skeleton with skin stretched across it. Oh but he had the sweetest little face with searching brown eyes. It was during that time, that his father's addiction, alcoholism and abuse were at their peak.

As devastating as those things were in my life, suddenly they did not matter anymore. Those things had caused enough problems and the very reason Joshua was in the world "too soon." *I could not focus on either my abuse or his father's addiction any longer. My baby boy was my priority - not my well-being and not his father's recovery. It's peculiar how sickness, adversity and yes even death become the great "equalizer" of all.* I had good job at that time, and most of all, comprehensive insurance that provided everything for my baby boy. I can assure you that if it had not, I would've given away every possession, and used every penny of my income to insure that my son was given every chance to overcome these obstacles. Every day was a gift.

Why is it that we human beings have to face such adversity to understand such a concept? Do we really have to come to the end of life or at the very least the end of "ourselves" to understand? We truly are kindred spirits, brothers and sisters, bearing remarkable resemblances of one another. Given that, the fact that any of us ever struggle with our self-esteem or our place in life seems a bit ridiculous. It seems ludicrous that we squabble and fight for prestige, for power, for authority etc. when we are all "family." We spend our whole lives with selfish ambitions, excessive consumptions and pretentious goals and for what? Security? Safety? At the end of it all, the last breath is drawn, we are stripped naked and bare, lying still in a box and buried deep beneath the earth. Rich, poor, great and small... we all meet the same fate. We meet our Maker on equal ground. We come in the world with nothing and we leave with nothing. The only things that matter are the treasures, the true treasures we leave behind. Anything tangible along the way is just a means to an end to love and care for those around us. The more we acquire the more we can contribute. Watching my friend Mitzi and her family through her last months was a stark reminder to me just what a gift each day is, and what a treasure those we have been given to share them with are to me. Many days in my own life when I didn't know if I would live or die, if my baby boy would live to push out another breath; watching his father, abuse his own life to the very end and watching other family members transition from this life to the next, have all be like the mirror of truth concerning what matters and what doesn't in this life. The sum total of my life experiences has been one reminder after another. We spend so much of life getting "wrapped around the axles" of circumstance and situation rather than focusing on those who are there with us during it all. Sadly, sometimes we don't realize their value and worth until they are no longer with us. Yes, adversity, sickness and death are all great equalizers. We come to understand what matters and what does not. After twenty-one years since my son's birth, I still view every day as a gift. His life is a gift; my life is a gift. Even if I do acquire possessions and wealth to leave behind, I hope that I leave behind treasures that can't be measured in dollars and cents. Regardless of the tangible riches that I may or may not be able to pass down to my son, I will have given him the greatest treasures of all - my time and love. Through it all, I pray that my son understands true value and true generosity. Generosity is not giving out of one's abundance but out of one's necessity. When Josh thinks of his mom, I hope treasures immeasurable permeate his mind - the sound of laughter on a lazy Saturday morning ringing in his ear, the smell of warm cookies arousing his senses, the twinkle of Christmas lights warming his soul and the arms of love reaching deep into his heart with comfort and encouragement. My hope is that all of these intangible treasures are passed down to his children one day. I don't want to ever take anything for granted, and I don't want him to take anything for granted either. Every day is a gift; every moment one heart touches another is a treasure. The more I reflect back on my life and all that I have come through, the more I understand the lessons my life has taught me. I realize even more just how blessed I truly have been and how blessed I am. The hurts and pains in my life were, at times, reminders of what was good so that I would not take them for granted and forget, and at other times, were hurdles strengthening my gratitude in and through adversity. Yes, I am truly blessed. Tonight in my heart I am as rich as Bill Gates. I am rich and not just in "name" only!

CHAPTER 30

LET IT GO!

"I held on to my companions so tightly because I was so afraid of rejection. I held on to rituals in my life, because my life had been so out of control and change petrified me. I held on to my feelings, thinking that if I expressed them, I would be viewed as an emotional wreck."

Almost two years ago, I received a long awaited "miracle" - a new house. One thing about moving, you never truly realize just how much "stuff" has been accumulated until you have to pack it all up. I've always tried to be good about triaging things over time and not holding on to items that I do not use, but like everyone, I find it hard sometimes to let go of things. We rationalize saying we might use that item one more time. If it is clothing, we say perhaps it will be back in style "one day" or we may lose the weight and be able to wear something too small again "one day." Somehow, "one day" never comes; we hoard useless junk that we deceive ourselves into thinking was treasure. My brother was the poster child for such activity. When he was a little boy, we would walk to and from the bus stop each day before and after school. Craig had one of those little school boxes like we all had. You know the ones - the boxes that mimicked the old "cigar boxes." How I loved getting my little school box each year and filling it with my new school supplies - a ruler, glue, crayons, pencils and scissors. My scissors were unique in that I was left-handed so I had to get special scissors. Being left-handed is a story for another day, but back to my little brother. Craig had all of the usual items in his box but by mid-semester of the year, his box was crammed with so much more. You see, my brother saw "everything" as treasure. When we would walk home or walk to the bus stop, anything that was shiny or unique along the roadside was a rare find for Craig. He would cram his little box full of bottle tops, torn pieces of paper; you name it, and he had it in that little box! He never threw anything away. To this day at age fifty-one, he still holds on to things. My mom is kind of the same way. There is just some strange sense of security in keeping things. Not just sentimental things but things that seemingly to the rest of us have no value at all. Truly, some of those items are of no value. It's just that they both struggle with letting them go.

It seems strange. I pride myself on being able to discard items that I have not used in sometime - giving them away to others that can use them or donating them to thrift stores etc. That is... with tangible things. Oh how I've held on to things not so tangible over the years! Hurts, disappointments, fears, insecurities, habits, patterns, friendships and affections... I suppose we all do that in one way or another. Even the bad things become like a security blanket for us. It isn't that they are good for us; it's just that they are familiar and we tend to get stuck in the familiar. It is comfortable and we convince ourselves we would be losing something by letting them go. We would lose our freedom or our hearts, our emotions or a million things in between. We hang on to unhealthy emotions, to destructive habits and patterns, addictions and vices; we find a safe haven in the den of so called friends who drag us down and make it way too easy to stay stuck in that place of limbo in our lives. We rationalize again and again. *"But it's just the way I am." "They were there for me when things fell apart." "I'm not judged when I'm there." "It makes me feel better about myself."* Yes, we find a million reasons to hang on thinking we are free and independent by doing so, when in truth, we are more bound than ever. Oh the price we sometimes pay for what we see as "freedom."

Negative things and emotions aren't the only things we hang on to that can hold us back or trap us up in someway. Sometimes, insecurities, fears or narrow-mindedness causes one to hold too tightly to love or to friendship, to tradition or structure, to success or authority. All of those things in and of themselves are good, but can become vices or obsessions and even distractions from what matters. Have you read the statement *"love with an open hand, not a closed fist?"* It is a sage piece of advice. Love needs room to grow. Friendships need freedom to flourish, traditions need space to change as life situations change; Success needs opportunity to diversify. We are diminishing the value of the people and things in our lives by holding on too tightly. The art of "letting go" is a valuable lesson in trust - for the process of life, for others, for oneself, and for God.

It has taken me long periods of retrospection and past losses to fully understand just how tightly I had been holding on to everything. *I held on to my companions so tightly because I was so afraid of rejection. I held on to rituals in my life, because my life had been so out of control and change petrified me. I held on to my feelings, thinking that if I expressed them, I would be viewed as an emotional wreck.* I did not realize the freedom that would have come by simply letting go and letting life "be." My heart and soul struggled with the freedom to dance and sing, to run and soar. I lived way below my promise and privilege from my Maker for so many years. Trust was a difficult step for me. Without trust, life is simply a long road of existence, when it should be an adventure.

Several years ago, I read a story about the trapping of monkeys over in Africa. There is a certain monkey that the natives hunt and trap. The hunting method is not what one would expect. They aren't captured with nets, spears, guns or any such method, but are ensnared by their own devices. The natives take gourds and hollow them out, then they cut a small hole just big enough for the monkey to stick his small hand in. The gourd is then filled with nuts and delicacies which the monkey craves. All the natives have to do is sit back and allow the monkey room to imprison himself. Hiding in the brush, the natives watch as the monkey - like "Curious George" comes along following the aromatic scent of the nuts and fruits, curious about the strange hollowed out gourd and soon the natives' prey is captured. Each time, the monkey will stick his greedy hand in the gourd and grab as many of the nuts and fruits as he can, but to his dismay, finds that he cannot remove his hand from the small opening in the gourd because it is no longer big enough. All the monkey has to do is let go of his "treasure" and he is free. Driven by his appetite and greed, the monkey never thinks to let go of the nuts and is imprisoned and doomed.

We really are often the same way. Time and time again it would be so simple. There is that voice whispering inside *"let it go."* Still, we refuse to listen. The voice is louder still… *"Let It Go,"* but still we hold on to people, to activities, to hurts, to possessions. Over time, the voice grows even louder… *"LET IT GO!"* Truly the whole universe screams out at us in various ways through circumstance after circumstance not wanting us to wait until tragedy, or disaster, until there is health repercussions, or until we push away the very ones who love us most before we "get a clue." It really is true. Sometimes we do not realize what we have until it is gone. As I look at this beautiful home I have been blessed with, I reflect on the road traveled getting here. I realize… I could've been on this road "home" so much sooner.

CHAPTER 31

A TRIP TO PARIS

"I, too, had been to 'Paris' - more than once. I had learned how to control my 'fear of flying' and learned much about various ways of life far different from my own. I had learned every social, romantic, emotional and spiritual 'etiquette' in the book and spent years on my soapbox sharing what I had learned with others."

When I began preparing for my move to my new house, I was talking with my family about setting up my piano in the house. It had been in storage for a few years and I was truly looking forward to playing it again. On days when life had swept in with a vengeance, I could always sit at that familiar place, stroll across the keys and find a place of rest and peace for a few moments. It was my escape. I could take myself to a far away location without ever leaving my living room. I had discovered this special power of music when I was just a young girl. My fingers would walk across the ivories on my piano and before long, I was far, far away from our paneled living room on Riverside Drive. On days when I was hurt over unkind words or felt ignored by someone, when I doubted my own self-worth or felt as if I had not met the expectations of others, I could pour every ounce of emotion out on those keys and when I did, it was like fuel in a jet engine - and the piano was my ticket to fly away from my troubles for a moment. I could pretend I was in some exotic location around the world or a beautiful city of culture like Athens or maybe Paris. Music gave me wings to fly, not only far away, but high above my struggles.

The day finally came - moving day, and that same piano I had as a child and played my first note on, was set up in my beautiful new home. I felt as if an old friend was back home with me. Actually, I felt as if "I" was home. Having that place of refuge that had been mine for so many years as a part of my new house, truly made it feel like home. When I sat down at the keyboard, I placed my long, skinny fingers on the ivories and it was as if I had never been away. Josh was amazed that I could play as well as I did, and that I still remembered so many musical pieces. It had been such a long time since I had moved my hands across the keys. When he left me alone with my music, tears began to stream down my face and splatter the ivories. The house itself was a miracle and an outward symbol of an internal journey for me.

About a month after I moved into my home, I invited my grandmother over, as she had not seen the house since it was set up and decorated. Almost as soon as she got there, she made her way over to the piano and began to play and to sing! Maw Maw Weeks has and always will be my inspiration. No one rivals her zest for life, her calmness of spirit, her confidence and childlike faith. She simply loves life! It had been awhile since I had heard her play, but she took to the keyboard like a duck to water and delighted and amazed us. She has been my biggest cheerleader in life and music was just one of the many things she encouraged me to always share with others. She is one to offer no excuses for "hiding talent under a bushel." She expects nothing less than for all of us to "let it shine." She is the greatest example of what it truly means to be a person of character and right spirit, and to be a success in life. She holds nothing back. She gives it her all no matter what she is doing. She is absolutely amazing. When she was sixty-something, she decided to take piano lessons. My grandmother had played by "ear" her whole life, but took on the challenge of learning to read music at that age. There she was that day in my home, almost ninety, playing and singing with the delight of a child. There is nothing quite like seeing your "granny" going to town on the piano! She definitely was tickling the ivories that day. My grandmother is always stretching and growing, stretching and growing and re-discovering herself along the way no matter how old she gets. I don't recall what she played and sang that day, but to me they were love songs straight from the heart. Watching her play and even sing a little song, it seemed that for a moment, she was also in her own world - lost in melody and memories. I imagined her singing her little song with Paw Paw in years gone by in one of their churches. I could almost see her as a young teen bride, riding by Paw Paw's side in an old coal truck as they went door to door selling coal. I just kind of think she might've hummed a tune or two as they drove from place to place along highways and old country roads. The thing about Maw Maw's travels was she always learned something on the journey. She seemed wiser with each passing day to me and her song became sweeter through the years.

I wasn't so sure if I had returned from my voyages around the "world" any wiser at all. Remember my favorite movie character? I often felt like Sabrina. She traveled to Paris to escape a fearful, hurting and insecure heart. After much time there, she grew from a shy young girl, to a sophisticated lovely young woman. Yet with all that she had discovered, the one thing she had not learned was to trust and cherish the one valuable that she took with her - her pure and lovely heart. I've shared her words before, but will share them again. She stated that she came back from Paris *"stupider than ever."* **I, too, had been to "Paris" - more than once. I had learned how to control my "fear of flying" and learned much about various ways of life far different from my own. I had learned every social, romantic, emotional and spiritual "etiquette" in the book and spent years on my soapbox sharing what I had learned with others.** In addition, I had allowed the music that had taken me on the journey inside my own heart play a melody sweet to the ears of those I loved, but often could not hear it in my own ear. Sitting in my new home at that old piano, I realized that my heart's song had not touched my soul in a very long time. While I did feel as though I had come "home" that day as I played that serene melody after moving in to my house, there were still some lessons to be learned. Yes, I had come "home," but had not unpacked all the baggage just yet. In search of answers, I didn't just glide my hands across the piano keys, but across computer keys. The days and months that followed - up until the writing of this very chapter, took me even further on my journey. Rather than listening to my heart's song, I had listened to other songs play as an escape from hurts that I had not wanted to face. I experienced more steps in the "relationship dance" and listened to the alluring song of companionship one more time, convincing myself that it would soothe my heart. For the record, it didn't. At long last, I discovered that my heart could not dance to the rhythm of a heart that did not beat in sync with my own, nor could it sing in harmony to a song with no melody. Not every heart you meet is ready for love. Two hearts must have a love that is in tune with each other in order for their lives together to become a symphony. Understanding this intellectually is simple, but grasping it emotionally is still such a process. There is much truth to the statement *"the heart wants what the heart wants."* It takes awhile to convince the heart what the mind and spirit already know. I am learning to be more patient with myself through this process though some days, I shake my head with wonder at how slow I have been to learn such a simple lesson concerning life and love!

Now that I have returned from a round trip in my most recent "flight of heart," I think I too, have come back from my own "Paris" also *"stupider than ever"* in some ways, but even that brings a smile to my face. The one thing I have not lost is my capacity to love with a pure heart regardless if others can reciprocate that love, loyalty, trust and respect. I do feel just a measure of sadness when the same love and loyalty that I have shown has not been shown to me, but you see, it has never been about whether the other person shows me love, loyalty and respect or treasures me. What matters is whether or not I show these things to myself. When I love and respect myself as much as I do others, many of the heartaches that could occur won't - simply because I won't allow myself to be treated as anything less than a valuable treasure. Love's journey does not begin when another person falls in love with you. It begins when you fall in love with yourself. Such love, self respect, self-esteem and self-care actually creates a more loving atmosphere with others. *"To acquire wisdom is to love oneself; people who cherish understanding will prosper."* This is the lesson traveling to "Paris" has taught me and the lesson that has brought me "home" through this long process. Tonight the sweet song in my heart plays once again.

CHAPTER 32

COMING HOME

"...we all started singing. As we sang about 'heaven,' Aunt Betty's eyes opened for just a moment and she looked up and then a tear trickled down that pale sunken cheek. She saw something we could not see. She saw 'home...'"

I am a Hallmark Channel fan. I confess. I love sappy movies with touching endings. Hallmark movies always leave your heart with a warm glow. Early fall before last, I watched a true story on Hallmark about a dog by the name of Hachi. Hachi was the epitome of loyalty, even for a dog. Every day he would walk his master to the train station as he left for work and every day he would return to meet him. He sat through snow, rain, heat and cold - faithfully waiting. One day Hachi did not want to go to the train station with his master. He tried everything he knew to detain him and keep him home. Still, his master left for the day. Later that day, Hachi's "reason" was revealed. His master, while teaching a music class at the university, fell with a heart attack and died. The story unfolded to reveal Hachi struggling to accept what had happened. Even after being sent to live with his master's daughter and her husband, Hachi still felt that strong sense of loyalty to his master. As the story progressed, Hachi ended up running away from their home, living under the railroad tracks and faithfully going to the train station every day to "wait" for his master to "come home." It wasn't until Hachi "came home" himself that they were "reunited."

After I watched this moving in that same fall season several years ago, I spent time with family members working at my aunt's house preparing things for her and her family to move in to their new home. This task of love was much more than routinely helping out a family member. You see, my aunt Betty was scheduled for surgery that week - a mastectomy after a third bout with breast/bone cancer. She was in her mid-sixties, was a pastor's wife and had spent her whole adult life living in homes belonging to others - in parsonages of the churches they pastored. She had never once had a house that she could truly and completely call "home." Through all of the issues that she was facing, she was finally receiving the chance to experience her own home for the first time ever. One day, Mom and I took Maw Maw Weeks over to the house to prepare for Aunt Betty's "homecoming." We met her son Anthony and his wife Trish there to hurriedly clean and straighten up before she arrived. Aunt Betty's family had spent two days moving her furniture, setting everything up and getting the house ready for she and my uncle. We set up floral arrangements, cookie jars, fruit bowls... decorative towels were hung, comforters spread on the beds, pillows tossed about and floor rugs strategically placed. The house smelled of freshly lit candles and hot soup simmering on the stove. After leaving the hospital, Aunt Betty was speaking with my mom. Even after major surgery she was "giddy." *"Where are you?"* my mother asked. *"I am coming HOME to my house!"* Aunt Betty explained... Coming home - for the first time ever she could say those words. The following day, Aunt Betty shared about her first morning "home." She said that they woke up, sat out on their back porch looking out over their land. *"I sat there and cried,"* she said. The realization of truly being at home had overwhelmed her.

Aunt Betty had been like that loyal dog Hachi. She had loved and served others, served God and waited every day to see the fruits of her labor. She had never stopped believing that one day all she longed for would "come home" to her. Even after three bouts with cancer, she stood strong fully accepting the divine plan and purpose for her life. Finally, all of those things she had been waiting for did not come home to her, but she "came home" to them! This "homecoming" was short-lived for my sweet aunt, however. Life did not smooth out as she had hoped it would in their retirement. Life never really does, I suppose. Her husband was very ill and over the course of the months that followed, he went down hill rapidly until he took his last breath. During those months, my aunt once again pushed aside her own needs to be by his side. Aunt Betty stayed strong, faithful, committed, grateful, and never once lost her gratitude. As time progressed, Aunt Betty continued to fight her final bout with cancer, remaining ever faithful and living each day with thanks. The months rolled on and Aunt Betty's body continued to dwindle away, but her spirit and great heart remained stronger than ever. She never gave up, she never lost faith and she expressed love and gratitude with every breath even when that breath became labored. I wonder. Do I have that kind of tenacity? That kind of childlike trust and faith? I, too, felt like I had been waiting to "come home" my whole life. Along the journey, I had always wanted to be ever so loyal, so faithful, so tenacious to go out each day, serving and loving, waiting and expecting. It is that desire that has led me "home." It has now been a year and a half since I moved into the new house that miraculously was given to me, but even though I call it "home," this house made of bricks and mortar is not really "home." The meaning is much deeper, I sense. Aunt Betty taught me this.

A year and half passed from the day we moved Aunt Betty into her home and about six months after I moved into my home. Each week over the months, the reports on Aunt Betty were not good. She was losing this battle with her cancer. We all got to that point to where we prayed that her suffering would end. Yes, we prayed for healing, but she had taught us that healing came in many forms. One day, I was talking to a friend of mine on the phone about how hard it was to watch her suffer. I told my friend Billie that I felt Aunt Betty was hanging on for something or someone. She paused a moment and said *"have you thought that someone might be you?"* My heart broke. I knew what I had to do. That afternoon, I left work, hopped in my car and headed down the interstate on that long drive to her home in the country. When I arrived, she was already incoherent, at least from what we could tell. I approached her bed, held her hand and kissed her on the cheek and told her how much I loved her. I sat and waited with Mom, my aunt and uncle, my cousins and Maw Maw. A minister came and prayed with us, and read scripture over her. Then, *we all started singing. As we sang about "heaven," Aunt Betty's eyes opened for just a moment and she looked up and then a tear trickled down that pale sunken cheek. She saw something we could not see. She saw "home"* - her true final home in the distance and the face of the One who had been with her every step of the way waiting there to welcome her home one more time. I believe she also saw my uncle and Paw Paw waiting there too. It had been way too long since they had been separated from their wife and daughter. In less than an hour of my arrival, Aunt Betty went "home." Yes, she was waiting on someone, she was waiting on me with a final lesson that she needed to teach me. Watching this precious woman move from her home here to her eternal home, left me no doubts about where and what "home" truly is. Home isn't this beautiful house that I have been given. It is my faith, my tenacity, my serving, my loving and my expectation that "is" my "home." Who we are really does not rest in the things we do, or the things we possess. Those things can change every day and often do. Who we are still resides even if everything external is stripped away. Perhaps I finally understand. "Home" is truly just a heartbeat away…

CHAPTER 33

CHRISTMAS GIFT!

"Somewhere around midnight, we would wind our way up that mountainous country road and in the distance see her yellow porch light burning. It was guiding us home like a beacon in the night."

If I were to mention the name "Madea" it would be a familiar movie character for many. Madea's clan portrays characteristics of "family" that many of us would deny or at least choose to forget! Madea's family is anything but normal. The truth is, there is no "normal" concerning family as each family has its own quirks and idiosyncrasies. I suspect that Madea's family and each of our families have more in common than we would admit. Everyone has that loud or obnoxious relative. There is at least one uncle who wears plaid pants from the seventies or an aunt with the nauseating dime store perfume. Invariably we all have that cousin or sibling who has accomplished more than any of us combined and will remind everyone of it as often as possible, lest we forget. There is always that beautiful niece or sister or cousin with the hour glass shape and the silky long hair that everyone loves to hate. We think of at least one cuddly lap we all loved to crawl into as a child and one broad shoulder we ran to for crying on. Family members are the first people we can't wait to leave behind when we grow up and the first one's we can't wait to return home to once we do. Family is our practice field for life. The power of love and family can never be over estimated. Also, family comes in all shapes and sizes and doesn't always require a "blood" connection to constitute "family."

A few years ago, I attended our annual family reunion. Actually, it was the first one that I have attended since this tradition started several years ago. As I spent time with each of my relatives, we tried to determine exactly how long it had been since I had been up to visit. Much to my surprise, it had been seven years! The one thing I found, after all this time, was just how far love reaches across time and space. We are family and that bond is ever present no matter how long or how far apart we are. What a soul cleansing few days this was for me. In a matter of days, it seems that love covered a lifetime of issues. I looked at one of my cousin's who had lost his wife to cancer some time ago. He had totally changed his course in life to pursue a vocation that would allow him to take his own hurt, grief and loss and use it as a catalyst for good in the lives of others. He is now a minister. I listened to another cousin as he stood in front of all the family and spoke of his life struggles from disease. Even in adversity, he was encouraging others. I took to heart the sobering news from my cousin's husband who had a daughter facing surgery due to cancer in her body. They had put aside their own adversity to open their home up to us for the weekend. I chatted briefly with other cousins who had experienced the pain that only those who have gone through a divorce understand. They, too, stood with a smile on their faces and a message of hope in their hearts to others facing similar situations. This is truly what "reunion" is all about "a coming together of people who have been divided…" Divided by what? By time, space, circumstances and a million other things. In this "coming together" we were reminded again just how much love covers and it truly does abound in "family" regardless of who your family is. Sometimes it is those blood relatives and sometimes those brothers and sisters of the heart.

On our drive back from dinner one evening, I sat between two of my cousins who love to "hate" each other. By that I mean they like to pick on each other. I suppose I was taking my life in my own hands. One of those cousins has been privy to secrets I've shared with her and the other one is the boy who used to be "the pincher" in our family when he was a child. If you didn't look him in the eye when you were talking to him and he felt you were ignoring him, he would grab the softest skin part of your neck and pinch the "fire" out of you - (another southern term). Here I was between "a rock and a hard place"… one could hurt me physically and the other emotionally! Whew… By the time we arrived back to my aunt's I had laughed until my side hurt. They could talk about each other but I assure you, if someone else outside of family talked about either one of them, they would've jumped on that person like a mama bear protecting her cubs. You know the old adage *"I can talk about family, but don't you dare talk about them!"* Love truly does cover all. The next day at the reunion, I stood between the two of them one more time as the three of us sang *"Amazing Grace."* Love, grace and mercy had brought us all together one more time. Family portrays the love of our Maker like nothing else. The ones who know us best still love us most. That is love that comes straight from the heart of God.

When I was a little girl, I could not wait for our seasonal trips to Mama Rich's and Paw Paw's house. Usually, we would leave at the end of a day after my parents finished a work day. This meant that we would not arrive until midnight or so to Mama Rich's house. She would always tell us that she would go to bed for awhile until we arrived and would leave the porch light on. She was extremely hard of hearing, so she would actually wait for us in her living room so that she would be able to hear us when we drove up and rang the bell. I don't really think she ever slept. She was as excited as we were. *Somewhere around midnight, we would wind our way up that mountainous country road and in the distance see her yellow porch light burning. It was guiding us home like a beacon in the night.* Family is kind of like Mama Rich's porch light. No matter how far apart we are or how long it has been since we've been together, family always has that porch light on watching and waiting and welcoming home. What a reunion we would have with Mama Rich that midnight hour. We would wearily straggle in, we kids would wipe the sleep from our eyes after sleeping for miles on the road; Mama Rich would crack a sleepy smile across her tired face and then she would shout *"Christmas Gift!"* I never really understood what that greeting meant until adulthood. With her, every visit from her loved ones was like Christmas. It was a gift for her no matter the time of year. I hope she knew what a gift those moments were for us.

I would not trade that family reunion experience for all the treasures in the world. Yes, I was reunited with family, but mostly, I was reunited with myself. I came back to my roots, once again, as we talked about childhood memories and shared adult burdens and joys. Tonight as I reminisce about that family reunion, the days are actually counting down until Christmas in my new home. I am snuggled up on my sofa, with nothing but the quiet of the night playing in my ear and the song of love dancing in my heart. I am watching the glow of the twinkling lights on my Christmas tree welcoming me "home" like Mama Rich's porch light. Each sparkling light reminds me of days gone by, of the love of family, the loyalty of friends, the blessings that have come through faith, patience and perseverance, and those twinkling lights are a symbol of hope for my future like the star that led the wise men to the hope of the world. Their glow warms me deep inside, melting away unspeakable pains and hurts from the past. I can still hear Mama Rich's welcome ringing in my ears - *"Christmas Gift!"* Yes I truly have come home!

CHAPTER 34

THE END OF THE BEGINNING

"I am home - forever home in a place called 'acceptance' - a place I have longed to dwell always it seems. How ironic - it is the one thing I had been searching for my whole life and really had all along."

The longer I write, the more I realize that there is no stopping place. Years ago I played a piano piece that was entitled *"The End Of The Beginning."* It was a musical interpretation of how it might sound at the end of our age when we find ourselves in our eternal home in the universe facing "forever." The one thing I recall about that piece is that the final notes faded into an arpeggio across the keys that sounded like the final destination was one of peace. While I can't explain it, the "arpeggios" running up and down this computer keyboard sound much the same to me. With each word, I sense that they are stretching across time and space to a place of peace.

Since I began writing this book over four years ago, I have experienced another lifetime of ups and downs it seems. Yet, as I sit wrapped tightly in this seatbelt of "love" on this ride we call "life," I understand that my journey has not ended and never will until I take my final breath. For the first time, I am not afraid of the "ride" because my destination is not a place that man can define but a place that my Creator divinely built before I was born - a place deep inside my heart where His essence lives and love resides. Today, the one thing I realize is that I have not been on this journey alone, no matter how many times I felt alone. Loneliness is not a state of being but a state of mind and emotion deep inside. No, I have never truly been alone! I think of my aunt Betty through her final stages of cancer, of my son Josh who continues to find his way and who is in the process of spreading his wings which may very well take him far away from me at some point. I think of my 91 year old grandmother Maw Maw Weeks who enjoyed another Christmas with us and how we are looking forward to another one soon, and I wonder how many more years of blessing we will have with her. I think of my parents who both battle health issues that could lead them on a different leg in the journey at some point. As I think of each of them and others with me in this journey, my heart grieves over inevitable loss and yet is full all at the same time. I must allow all of these emotions to fill my love tank if I am to continue this journey. Yes, I grieve because the day most surely will come when like Aunt Betty, Maw Maw Weeks and my parents will go "home" - the day will arrive when Josh will move far away, and each day that I face a new dawn, I encounter questions, changes and transitions - all of which inevitably will bring hurt, sadness and disappointment just as surely as they bring joy, happiness and fulfillment. One cannot circumvent the great "circle of life." So with all of this, what I understand through my emotions and my tears, is that each person near and dear to me will be where they need to be along life's timeline and I will be where I am - where I am divinely placed, loving them and carrying them in my heart. My "home" is here, not in my new house but here inside this petite body, right in the middle of my heart. *I am home - forever home in a place called "acceptance" - a place I have longed to dwell always it seems. How ironic - it is the one thing I had been searching for my whole life and really had all along.* My Divine "Father" loves and accepts me! Just as He does, so I can love and accept myself and receive the love and acceptance of others. Even more, I now have the capacity to give others that love and acceptance out of a full heart that is no longer void, no longer searching. Oh, if I had only realized this long, long ago! But my Creator, in His patience, never gave up and kept pursuing me no matter how far I strayed, how much I hurt, how fearful I became or angry I behaved. All of creation and the universe kept giving me signs and clues along the way desperately trying to lead me "home." My family and friends displayed that same divine patience and love, standing at the end of the road watching for my "return."   For that, I am forever grateful and humbled. How deceived I had been even in my own heart.   I thought I was tolerant and loving!   I thought it was perpetrators of hurt and pain in my life who were not. It takes awhile to understand that the only person we can "fix" is us, and the only person responsible for our happiness is the one staring back at us in the mirror each day. No matter what comes our way we have a choice as to what we do with it and about it. This journey to find myself began and is ending here in my own heart.

So many years, so many experiences… I realize that each of them, good and bad, have led me to where I am now and made me who I am today. It really is no longer necessary for me to stretch across the corridors of my past or even reach towards the path of my future to determine who or what I am or who or what I should be. I can find that all in this moment of time because of God's divine love that is displayed to me through tangible hands and hearts of those who mean the world to me. I can look into the tear-stained eyes of my son and feel the compassion of God Himself who is touched by the hurts and pains in my life. It is in my son's eyes that I see myself - the mom. who years ago cried many tears as this young man came into the world too soon and fought his own physical battle. He has cried a few tears for my battles through the years without a doubt. I can look into the loving eyes of friends in my life and find a place of belonging and acceptance. It is there that I see the woman with the huge heart who longs to be that safe place for others close to me just as they have been for me. I can hear my mom and dad's heartfelt prayer for blessing in my life and come face to face with the essence of abundance - a divine Father who provides for my every need and guides me along my journey teaching me the many roads to success and blessing. With my parents' prayer, I hear that determined woman inside saying *"I will never give up!"*

Just last week, I read words out of a passage of scripture in Isaiah 46 that mean even more to me today. I even printed them and posted them on the side of my computer at work. *"I have cared for you since you were born. Yes, I carried you before you were born. I will be your God throughout your lifetime - until your hair is white with age. I made you, and I will care for you. I will carry you along and save you. Remember the things I have done in the past. For I alone am God! I am God, and there is none like me. Only I can tell you the future before it even happens. Everything I plan will come to pass, for I do whatever I wish... I have said what I would do, and I will do it... For I am ready to set things right, not in the distant future, but right now!"*

I believe with every fiber of my being that there is divine guidance in life for all of us. We simply must acknowledge that there is help higher than we are. As frail human beings. we have been given a great gift - supernatural power and strength, guidance and love. Our lives will reflect whether or not we accept that or not. A song is playing in my ear. *"Broken and spilled out... My most precious treasure lavished on Thee. Broken and spilled out and poured at Your feet. In sweet abandon let me be spilled out and used up for Thee."* This is a hymn of surrender, of transparency. We can never fully find ourselves until we rid ourselves of "self." Part of that metamorphosis involves shedding the skin of hurt and pain, of disappointment and failure, of grief and loss. That is the strange paradox of life. The more we let go of, the more we obtain; the more we give, the more we get; the more we seek, the greater treasures we will find. Like the woman who broke open her alabaster box and poured out her most precious treasure for Christ Jesus, I have opened my "alabaster box" and poured out my treasure - my heart, my life and all that I am or ever hope to be. Strangely, the emptiness that I felt when that "box" was still in tact is gone. Now that it is broken and poured out totally for love, I am filled up again. This time, not just with my own efforts, my own desires - but with the essence of God's divine love that has come to me from above, from within and from all around me through the hearts and hands of those who mean the world to me. I never have to feel alone. I never have to feel insignificant, unimportant or insecure, I never have to be afraid or live in turmoil. There is a place for me that was designed before I was even born - a place that no one can fill or fit into. Yes, this peace that has come through some rather tumultuous times is stirring deep inside. I found this peace in that safe, still place in the center of the flame where nothing is burned or consumed. It is here in this bubble of protection that I can hear the faint sound of music. The arpeggios of my heart are running up and down my soul as I write these words today. Somehow, I sense that with each word, I am stretching across time and space and fading into a beautiful place - a place of lasting peace that is mine, not just sporadically like in times past, but forever if I so choose.

"I started my journey as a woman searching for the little girl inside. Along the way though, I realized that the little girl was searching for the woman..."

Epilogue

I wish that I could complete the "rest of the story" now, but it is still a work in progress. My hands continue to write as my life's story unfolds a little more each day. There are no great open doors before me or profound moments to speak of. Doors open, others close, relationships ebb and flow and life goes on. New chapters unfold - new characters appear on the scene. Like my stories from yesterday and yesteryear, my days continue to be filled with ordinary moments... some beautiful and others dark and somber, but moments that create a harmony of life that is rich with experience and growth.

Joshua is continuing down his own path along life's journey. *"Son, no mother could be more proud of you than I am for all of the obstacles you've overcome in life to get to where you are today. Stay the course and stay true to yourself always. Mostly, listen to your heart because it is there that God whispers."* I am a mom who feels like a winner loving and laboring to help get Josh to this point. *"We did it together son!"* As many words as I write on pages daily, there are not enough words to express the joy I feel at being blessed with having Joshua as a son. He is an incredible young man. God knew exactly what I needed to give me a reason to wake up many days.

I have found a place of peace and acceptance through my family and feel more blessed than I truly deserve. *"Mom and Dad, Paula, Craig and Byron, Maw Maw Weeks, aunts, uncles and cousins... I could never offer enough words of gratitude for your love, your acceptance, your care, your prayers, your faith, your belief in me when I did not even believe in myself. What a heritage God has given me. Thank you from the bottom of my heart. Forgive me for the hurt that times in my life may have caused."* Now, my prayer is that the rest of my life will be spent giving back in a small measure what my family has given me. I love you all from the depths of my being!

Epilogue

As I start this new leg to my journey and write more chapters in life's journal, I am surrounded by a close circle of friends who have not only stood by me, but also walked along side of me. They have cheered me on, held me up and been the wind beneath my wings. *"I could mention each of you by name, but I think you know who you are - my sisters, big brothers and even sons and daughters of my heart. You have shared the best of yourselves with me and poured so much into me. Because of you, I have found strength I never knew I had! Thank you for capturing a glimpse of the dream in my heart and believing in it as much or even more than I have. You have shined a light on my path and helped me find my way."* I am forever grateful. I don't know where I would be without your love and support.

With each new chapter of life, what I am discovering most is that I am lingering in a place of peace that I hope to never leave. This was where I was lost so long ago and this is where I found myself again. All that I was, all that I am, and all that I hope to be, starts and ends here - in that sweet tender heart of a girl who was touched by the love of an incredible God so long ago. Life has changed, circumstances have changed, and I suppose I have changed, but the one thing that remains the same, is that love, divine love deep in my childlike heart! It is here that I am home once again. The peace that this place brings has come through the very tool I am using now… words - not from the mouth or desires of others but from my own heart. My heart tells me who I am, who I should be, where I should and shouldn't go, do or shouldn't do. Perhaps I would've come to this place long ago if I had only allowed those words to take up residence in all the rooms of my heart sooner. They are words straight from my Maker's heart to mine, I sense. These words that my heart whispers have silenced the noise and speak peace, true lasting peace.

After so many restless, long lonely nights, now I sleep like a baby - the first time in years, actually. I can't remember the last time I felt such peace

- such rest. Finding the courage to write this book is the reason, I am sure. These hands of mine have ushered me into a peace like I've never known through simple words straight from my heart. They have unlocked a place in me that was held prisoner for way too long. I look at these hands of mine one more time. What is it I see in them now? Strength beyond what I ever imagined. They have carried me back in time and catapulted me forward into eternity. Now, somewhere in between, they wrap me in a blanket of peace through the words that are woven throughout each page, forming a tapestry of love deep in my heart. In it all, some things have changed and others have remained exactly the same. For all that I am, all that I have been and all that I hope to be still and forever rest in these hands...

Starla

In Closing

First to you ladies... As I interact with others like myself entering mid-life, I realize that I am not the only woman who has struggled with her own identity through her formative years. Woman was created as the "heart" of family and relationships. She was created with a resilience that defies human logic; and with that "gift" comes responsibility that leaves her to sometimes feel a bit unsure, a bit lost in it all. No one would know by looking at her though. She faces the day with a smile on her face, handling monumental tasks with the ease of a professional. She leads her "troop" with confidence and authority and embraces those under her care with a love only God can equal. She embodies what it means to have courage - not an absence of fear, but a relentless determination to never give up. By virtue of the role she was born for, this tough and tender creation understands the importance of self-evaluation. She must change and grow! She is never more "herself" than today because each day she is creating who she is, evolving into who she should be. This is no easy task given the fact that she is her world's "constant" in the midst of ever changing circumstances. It is an even greater task if she has also been given the responsibility of keeping herself and her loved ones balanced in adverse situations. While the task is even more daunting, it is all the more necessary. She must find times of introspection, she must evolve and grow and become stronger, if for no other reason than survival.

When I first began to write this book, it began as a quest for understanding and acceptance of who I was, who I had been and what I was becoming following years of abuse in relationships. I had lost so much of myself. Because of my own experiences, I wanted so desperately to get on my soapbox to women as a way to protect them from what I had been through, and then to expose "bad men" in the process because of the pain that I had endured. Everything was so cut and dried for me. There were good men and there were bad men. I so wanted to point the finger at bad men and tell them what they needed to do to become good men. The more I wrote, the more exposed I became and I began to open my heart not to those who had done me wrong, but to myself. Like mirrors to the soul, I saw things in me that caused me to choose them in the first place. It wasn't that they needed to be more of a "man," but I needed to be more of a "woman." The only person I could fix was "me." A healthy "me" would choose wisely, walk confidently, act prudently and live abundantly. You see, I could point out all day long the faults of such men who hurt women. What would that change? Them? No. So, I began a journey towards change and growth a journey that started and ended in my own heart. I had played the role of "victim" much too long. Finally through some of the most gut-wrenching times of hurt and reflection I have come to understand. I am NOT a victim! I am a victor and can rise above anything that others have caused or that I have allowed. I want someone out there to get this in your mind and heart. Many of the things we go through are beyond our control, but others are simply because WE allow them. We become whittled down until we allow ourselves to be treated poorly. We become the "victim" taking no responsibility for our own lives and actions. People treat you how you allow them to treat you. So if you are tired of where you are, experiencing what you continue to experience, let today be a day of change, not of others or even circumstances, but of you! Realize what a treasure you are. You are worthy of the respect and honor intended, of the care and protection that is your birthright as a woman. Treat yourself with kindness and love, respect and care and the rest will follow. Forgive those who have wronged you and most of all, forgive yourself.

Next to you men... I know you aren't as verbal or transparent about hurt or pain, but it is real just the same. When a woman does you wrong sometimes it can be even uglier. I am a woman, but I confess, women can be nasty and vindictive. I've talked with several men over the last few years and the common thought from each of them is that when a man is hurt deeply in his heart it is much harder and takes a great deal longer for him to find a way to trust again. Perhaps because women are the heart of a relationship and when she takes that away from him, the hurt is deeper than one can imagine. My expression to you is this. If you have been hurt by a woman, believe it or not, there are some of us who understand. We really are kindred spirits. It is possible to trust again. That trust must begin in your own heart. It is possible to stop the cycle of hurt once and for all.

A word for us all... When we are hurt, we all tend to go into "survival mode" of sorts; either retreating and hiding, or lashing out to protect ourselves from more harm. But for all of us, we are left with a choice - be a victim or become a victor. This is not just true in romantic relationships but in all relationships. A friend may disappoint us, a co-worker may stab us in the back, a parent may be hurt by a wayward child or a child by an unstable parent. Pastors are hurt by critical church members, church members are taken for granted by self-absorbed pastors. Bosses are hurt by disloyal employees; employees are looked over by greedy, uncaring bosses. Neighbors refuse to be neighbors, children sometimes are brutally honest and family members can be our worst critic. Hurt breeds hurt. Fear breeds fear, and distrust breeds more distrust. There is a way to break the cycle! There is a way to step beyond the "victim's" mentality. For me it came at a fork in the road of my life. Sometimes we get to a point of no return. We can't go back and we can't go forward until we choose. We must choose a path one way or the other. My path came after another broken relationship, loss of a job, failing health. I had no choice but to look at the truth staring me in the face. I could not continue as I had. What I was doing was not working. The words that I had been "preaching" to others had to be more than words. I took a good long look at the woman staring back at me in the mirror and with relentless determination, my eyes and my heart were totally open, perhaps for the first time. My focus now is not so much on what I dislike in others, but in understanding what I dislike in myself - and further, doing something to change that. How did this change come? It came from getting "self" out of the way in order to be totally surrendered to my Creator and opening up to all life has for me. Opening up the deepest parts of my heart and soul with no reserve has allowed me to be totally "me" for the first time in a very long time. Now, I can look at those who have hurt me and done me wrong, not through my own hurting heart, but through the heart of Divine Love. Being able to show love and mercy and understanding to the very one's who have wronged me has not changed them, but me. Life has allowed difficulty like the mother eagle uses thorns in the nest, to strengthen my wings so I can fly and soar! I have found that precious treasure of trust that was lost so long ago. No, not for those who had abused my trust. The trust that I have found again began with my Maker and ended with me. By trusting God first and foremost, I can now trust myself to make wise decisions that will lead me to the proper people who are worthy of my trust and will protect and cherish my love. The sum of it all in life and relationships really is in that one word - "trust." If we do not trust totally we will always live one step short of the divine plan for us. If we do not trust ourselves we will live below our potential and outside of our purpose. If we do not trust others, fear will rob us of peaceful communion and perfect love. Trust is the key because without trust you cannot truly love and without love you do not live but merely exist. Through this renewal of trust, an amazing metamorphous has taken place in me. The caterpillar has released a butterfly! I have embraced forgiveness for those who have hurt me in any way. I realize that I cannot move forward without it because this book would never make it to the shelf. It would just be a work in progress. So now, instead of justice - I choose mercy, love and forgiveness. Forgiveness is a difficult but necessary step along our journey if we are to move forward at all. With this forgiveness also comes courage - courage to face a lifetime of hurt, a lifetime of fear, and to boldly stand in the face of it all and finally say "enough is enough." Ironically, this forgiveness not only embraces those who hurt me, but it embraces "me." I have finally forgiven myself and let go of things that I have been too afraid to face my whole life. Forgiveness is what has moved me from victim to victor and it will do the same for you...

From My Heart,
Starla

Final Note: For Women Only

I believe that some of you will relate closely to the stories you've just read. Don't wait until the last third of your life like I did to "get a clue." If you are suffering abuse, refuse to take it another minute - GET OUT! You are NOT a dime store trinket; you are NOT a possession, YOU ARE A TREASURE! If you have been abused in the past, the message is the same. You are worthy to be loved! Not just any kind of so called "love" but love that comes straight from the heart of the One who created you. This love will come to you as you begin to learn how to love yourself. God loves you so much. He created you in all of your uniqueness for a special purpose. He longs to lavish His love on you. This is what we all are truly searching for anyway. All other "loves" will come up short and empty without the love of our Maker. Divine Love comes to you in forms you least expect. It may come through a circle of close friends who stand shoulder to shoulder with you holding you up when you are too tired to stand alone. Sometimes, it is through the helping hands of family who reach out or down no matter where you are ready to lift you up and encourage you. Learn to recognize the many faces of love. Once you do, then romantic and companion love will find its way to your heart with much less effort.

Just this week, I was talking with someone close to me about their sister. They told me she had a "hatred for men" due to abusive situations in her past both with her father and former companions. How I longed to reach out to her. I understood her in a way that others could not. That "hatred" stemmed from so much more than those perpetrators of "hurt." It was much deeper than that; deep inside her own heart. This I know only too well. There is something about abuse that causes us to feel ashamed and dirty, ugly and unwanted. We do not receive love from the one we love and then find ourselves void of love, even for ourselves. I encourage you today, forgive those who have hurt you, and then most of all, forgive yourself. You are precious! I will be honest with you. This process takes courage, perhaps even more than you've had to muster during abuse. Still, it is necessary and you are not alone! Forgive, forgive, forgive, forgive! Don't let the pains of the past dictate your future.

Perhaps you have not been the victim of abuse at least in its rawest form but have experienced pain in relationships, not just once, but over and over without understanding "why." It is easy to believe that a broken relationship is all the other person's fault even when there is a pattern there. Believe me I know... been there, done that. We can find so many excuses as to why something didn't work or wasn't right and then when it happens again we can excuse and explain away our actions and the reasons for them. A friend sent me a quote recently that explains this behavior. It said, *"We all have the freedom to choose, and making up excuses is a choice too... An excuse is worse than a lie, for an excuse is a lie, guarded. We human beings make excuses all the time. We talk about what we want to change and make a million and one excuses as to why we cannot get what we want."*

Here is a truth I feel compelled to share. You attract the same type of person and attitudes that you are and have. If you feel insecure or unloved you will draw that kind of person to you. If you feel secure, loved, emotionally healthy and beautiful you will attract the same. If you feel you are unworthy of such a noble person who is emotionally healthy, physically appealing, spiritually mature, dedicated and disciplined then you probably will never have such a person in your life. Remember what I said in the beginning of this conversation - YOU ARE A TREASURE! You are worthy of the very best. You don't have to go through a series of relationships hoping something will change and wondering why it never does. YOU are the one who needs to change - your attitude about yourself. If you cannot love "you" then it is most likely that a quality person will ever come around to love you. Love breeds love. Respect breeds respect and it all starts and ends in your own heart.

To those of you who do have a man in your life. Respect him, honor him. Be his biggest cheerleader, greatest ally and number one fan. Never take him for granted. Spend less time worrying about how he can become a better man for you. Become a better woman for him and most definitely for yourself and God then the rest will follow. You are the heart of the relationship and home. Be that safe place.

To those young women who have yet to find that special someone to share life with - take your time. Don't settle, don't compromise because you think you aren't good enough or perhaps you feel that time is running out. Wait on that knight in shining armor. If he does come but falls off his horse, if his armor gets a bit rusty or if he never comes - love yourself! You're worth it. To say that you aren't worth it is to say that your Maker did a bad job in creating you. As I said before, He created you in all of your uniqueness for a special purpose. A man will NOT make you complete. Only Divine Love can do that. Loving your Creator and being loved by Him makes you ready for the love of a man. It also molds you into the woman you should be for that man and for yourself!

To every woman young and old who may be starting out or starting over. Hide your heart in the heart of Divine Love. A man who is truly ready for a woman like you will find you there! Finally, stay focused living your best life, listen to your heart and stay true to that voice inside. It is the whisper of the One who made you guiding you on your way. He is as close as the next heartbeat…

From My Heart To Yours,
Starla

Final Note: Just For Men

I don't deny the fact that woman is the most complicated of all creations, and yes, we are difficult sometimes. God knew what He was doing when He said *"it is not good for man to be alone."* With this gift of woman comes wisdom and desire to embrace her in all her beauty and complexity. Polish her like a precious diamond and you will have a jewel that will light up your world. If you can wax your car, shine your shoes, display a trophy, brag to your fishing or bowling buddies, pamper a pet, protect your investments, motivate your children and honor your parents - then uplifting your woman should be a cinch. She really isn't asking for you to understand her. Face it, you never will - not totally. What she is asking is that you protect and treasure her. She is not just your companion, she is your heart. God made her to be the heart of the relationship, family and home. When she suffers, everything hurts because she brings life and love in a way that is not possible without her.

Being a good man that a woman respects, honors and fulfills is not as complicated as it seems. Just be there - plain and simple. Listen when you don't have a clue. Nurture her with words, with small gestures like a flower that needs water and soil to survive and grow. Let her dig deep roots in your heart and soul. She will be there forever if you simply let her in. She doesn't want to control you or stifle you. Being responsible for children and the home is enough. She wants to believe in you, depend on you. Be that safe place for her, for it is there in her heart that you will find home. Part of the struggle in being the man you should be lies in allowing her to be the woman she was divinely designed to be. If she has liberty to be the unique woman she was created to be, your task of being just the right man for her is much easier. Read the proverbs about a contentious woman. No one wants to be around her! So in short, when your woman is happy, everyone is happy! There is nothing a woman won't do for a man who respects, treasures and protects her. She is God's heart to you; you are the Divine's embrace to her. Let her know through all the good and bad that you won't let go - ever. She is your anchor you are her harbor.

Let her be the first thing you think of in the morning and the last thing you acknowledge at night. Neither she nor you will ever stray as long as you place each other at the top of the priority list. You always have time for what is first on the list. Finally, find a way to overlook wrongs just like you do with your buddies, your co-workers, your kids. She isn't perfect and neither are you, but together you can be priceless.

From A Woman's Heart,
Starla

Final Note: On Behalf Of All The Children

I'm not sure how adults lose sight along the way, but sometimes they forget that children are people, too. Children and youth long to be heard and accepted, and are hurt when they are ignored or taken for granted. Like their mothers, they need a safe place to dwell and nurturing to grow. Like their fathers, they need freedom to explore and increasing responsibility to make them strong. This book would not have been a reality had it not been for the vision of my own son. His wisdom, candor, insight and unconditional love were like diamonds in the sand. Even when he was a small child, he exhibited understanding well beyond his years. Sometimes life's lessons are understood best through the uncensored eyes of a child. They tell it like it is. They forgive and forget, they trust and believe and they love - no matter what... they love unconditionally. Young people and little people need just the right balance of love and discipline, nurturing and independence. If we don't believe in them, how will they ever believe in themselves? If our world is a scary place, think how they must feel about their world. Let them know they matter and provide something they can be sure of in the midst of a frightening ever changing world.

Moms and dads, teachers and coaches, family members and neighbors, church members and friends, if you want to do something worthwhile, if you want your life to count for something and if you want to preserve what you have worked so hard for, invest into the greatest treasure there is - our children. They don't need more "stuff," more activities, they need YOU. Give them what they need most, your time and attention, your love and your care. Let them know they are worth it. If you are too busy to spend time with your children, grandchildren, neighborhood children, or church children… then you are too busy. What you invest in them today will reap dividends tomorrow and forever in their lives. A wise man once said that love is spelled "T-I-M-E." How true that is….

From A Mother's Heart,
Starla

About The Author

About The Author

Starla Rich is founder of *Encouragement Enterprises* an organization that began with a simple concept - an "encouragement movement" created as a venue to pay forward encouragement and hope she has received in her own life. It is Starla's passion and desire to give back what has been given to her through some of life's most difficult moments. In her own words: *"There is enough negative in the world, so it is my desire to spread something positive, to be a soft spot to land, a safe place for people to visit. No matter the difficulty, and regardless of the obstacles in life there is always a choice - those obstacles can be roadblocks or stepping stones! That is my message of hope and the reason I encourage you to 'never give up' no matter what comes your way. You can do this! It all starts and ends deep inside your own heart. Believe in yourself... You are a treasure and YOU ARE LOVED!!!"*

She invites everyone to join the "encouragement movement" with the belief that each life can make a difference in the lives of others. Her message in a nutshell is *"Together we can change a moment, change a day, change a life!"*

You can write Starla at:

support@encouragiumenterprises.net

Or visit online at: **www.encouragemententerprises.net**

Thanks for reading! If you enjoyed this book or found it useful I'd be very grateful if you'd post a short review on Amazon. Your support really does make a difference and I read all the reviews personally so I can get your feedback and make this book even better. Thanks again for your support!

Made in the USA
San Bernardino, CA
02 June 2016